How to Play Dungeons & Dragons

A Step-by-Step Guide for Beginners

Charles Goodwill

been derived from various sources. Please consult a licensed professional before attempting any techniques outlined in this book.

By reading this document, the reader agrees that under no circumstances is the author responsible for any losses, direct or indirect, that are incurred as a result of the use of the information contained within this document, including, but not limited to, errors, omissions, or inaccuracies.

Table of Contents

Introduction

So, you want to play *Dungeons & Dragons*? Maybe you've seen depictions of the game in episodes of *Stranger Things, Community,* or *The Big Bang Theory* and it made you curious about what playing the game is like in real life. You might even have seen or listened to streamed or recorded games like *Critical Role* or *The Adventure Zone* and had your interest piqued. Or maybe you've just heard so many stories from the guy next to you at school or work about his usual Wednesday-night campaign and have decided that you want to get in on the fun.

Whatever your reason, you've decided to try dipping your toe into the exciting world of tabletop roleplaying games. But, while this hobby can be not only fun, but also a potential source of personal development and positive life-change, getting started can often be confusing and difficult. Not only are there all kinds of rules to learn, but finding the right people to play with and learning how to understand the lingo that gets thrown around in these spaces can be challenging, especially if you are entering the hobby by yourself.

I know this because I've been there. I remember answering the Facebook status of a loose acquaintance from college asking if anyone wanted to play *Dungeons & Dragons*. She wanted to try running the game and in reply I received a copy of the Player's Handbook and instructions to read it, roll up a character, and meet up at her apartment the following weekend. Though I ultimately had a blast and was instantly hooked, I'd be lying if I said that I wasn't a bit overwhelmed as I pored through the rulebook, trying to figure out what exactly I'd gotten myself into.

This is not to knock the Player's Handbook. This book is not intended to replace the need for the official rules. If that were the case, I'd probably be guilty of some form of copyright infringement. Rather, my goal is to give you a more practical guide to the issues that new players often face when first trying out *Dungeons & Dragons*, both in-game and out. This means discussing not only the basics of the rules, but also looking at the supplies needed to play the game, how to find the right group, what to expect when you're at the table, and how you can further explore the world of *Dungeons & Dragons* and other roleplaying games once you're hooked. Along the way, you'll also learn a little bit about the history of the game, the jargon you'll be expected to know as you become more experienced, and even a few handy points and frequently misunderstood rules that even many veteran players get wrong.

We've got quite the adventure ahead of us, so let's get started.

Chapter 1: What is Dungeons & Dragons?

If you read the introduction, then you know that *Dungeons & Dragons*, also known colloquially as "*D&D*," is a tabletop fantasy roleplaying game. But, depending on who you are and your level of exposure to the gaming community, this definition may not explain much about the nature of playing *D&D*. What is the point of the game? Is there a winner? What does playing a game of *Dungeons & Dragons* actually entail?

To put it in the simplest terms, *Dungeons & Dragons* is a way of generating a story as a group through a gamified version of improvisation. Unlike most other games you may have played, there is no "winner" in *D&D*, rather the fun comes from the communal experience of telling a story and working together as a group. At the gaming table, each player in a *D&D* group or "party" portrays and controls a single character within the shared narrative. These characters, called player characters or "PCs," are typically (though not always!) adventuring heroes in a fantasy world full of monsters, dangers, and magic. Together, these characters undertake perilous quests in the name of fame, glory, and wealth.

The exception to the "one player, one character" rule is the Dungeon Master. The Dungeon Master, also called the "DM" or, less frequently, the "Game Master" or "GM," has a more complex role in the game. They are responsible for driving the narrative, as well as portraying all of the other characters that the heroes meet in their travels, referred to as non-player characters or "NPCs." In addition, they are expected to act as the referee and final arbiter of the rules of the game. If the other players are the stars of a movie, the DM is both the director and screenwriter.

Within the framework laid out by the DM, the players are free to explore the world of the game, interact with the people within it, and, most importantly, partake in the adventures that it offers, using their character's skills and abilities to surmount the challenges they face. The effort and difficulty involved in accomplishing these things is modeled via the use of dice. The roll of a die is used to simulate, for example, the charm needed to bribe a guard for information or the martial skill required to hit an orc with a broadsword. The number rolled is an indicator of how well the character's attempt works, with a higher result giving them a better outcome.

Obviously there is much more to the game than this and we'll get into the nuts and bolts later on in this book, but for now, these are the most important details to understand. But it doesn't answer the question of why people play *Dungeons & Dragons* and other games like it.

The Point of Dungeons & Dragons

One of the biggest questions that I get from people when they find out that I'm a *D&D* player is what the "point" of the game is. If you're not competing against the other players, then what enjoyment can you get out of a game? The answer to that question is going to be different for every single player. Part of the beauty of *Dungeons & Dragons* is that, though they may operate within the same basic rules framework, the actual experience at each table is unique. That said, there are a number of common reasons that long-time players cite for why they keep coming back week after week.

The Story

Particularly in its current incarnation, *Dungeons & Dragons* and other games of its type are different from other popular tabletop games like say, Monopoly or chess, in that there is a plot to it. By playing the game, you get to experience a story in a more personal and visceral way than watching a movie or television show. This can be even more immersive than a video game, in which the player also gets to experience a narrative as an active participant, because of the higher level of freedom and flexibility that *Dungeons & Dragons* affords when compared to even the most detailed video game RPG. Having a human being able to adjust the game world on the fly means that, if you play with a skilled DM, there's no limit to what you can try to do and the directions that the story can go in response to those choices.

The result of this is the ability to get lost in a story in a way that few other forms of media can match. Why would you choose to watch *Lord of the Rings* when you could experience it? This might sound like an exaggeration, but this statement is not as hyperbolic as you might expect. Neuroscientists have done research on what happens in the human brain while playing pen-and-paper roleplaying games and found that the memories formed around a gaming table are stored in the exact same way as memories formed by actual life experiences. As far as your brain is concerned, sitting around a kitchen table rolling dice pretending to have a swashbuckling adventure is practically the same thing as doing it for real.

The Community

You've probably experienced the difficulty in maintaining friendships as an adult. Once we leave high school and college behind, it becomes harder to find people who share common interests and experiences. For most people, the only regular socialization they get is connected to their work. This is bad news for you if, like many people, you don't enjoy your job and the people you work with.

This is why any self-help book will tell you that it's important to have a hobby, preferably one with a social component. This allows you the opportunity to connect with people of similar interests in an environment that is fun, sociable, and low-stress. I can speak to this from experience. Not only has playing *Dungeons & Dragons* brought me closer to existing friends, keeping us from drifting apart over the years as our careers and personal lives have developed and diverged, but it has also introduced me to many new people who I might never have gotten the opportunity to know otherwise. Now, might this also occur if I'd found a passion for tennis or bar trivia? Sure. But, if you are like me and are already inclined toward imaginative pursuits, *Dungeons & Dragons* makes for the ideal social hobby.

The Challenge

Though *Dungeons & Dragons* is not a competitive game in the traditional sense, that does not mean that it does not involve using strategy to overcome obstacles. *D&D* has its roots in competitive tabletop wargaming and, though the course of history has shifted the focus and culture around the game, combat within *Dungeons & Dragons* is still ultimately a competition between the players and the Dungeon

Master, albeit one that a good DM will have carefully calibrated to be in the players' favor while still requiring them to think tactically in order for their characters to get out of it unscathed.

There is, in fact, quite a bit of similarity between *Dungeons & Dragons* and the thrill of playing team sports. As a cooperative game, successful combat strategy in *D&D* is all about coordinating the strengths and weaknesses of both the players and their characters to have the best chance at overcoming the obstacles and challenges posed by the Dungeon Master. In the same way that the linebackers are the biggest, strongest guys on a football team, the PC with the most hit points, usually a Barbarian, Fighter, or Paladin, is the one you want going toe-to-toe with a dragon, taking the big hits and locking it down while the other members of the party can pepper it with spells and keep the front line from being taken out before the dragon's been slain. It's not quite the same kind of competition as in a more traditional board or card game, but the potential for complex strategy and the satisfaction that comes with it still absolutely exists in a *Dungeons & Dragons* session.

A Brief History of D&D

One of the most intimidating things about *Dungeons & Dragons* is the richness of the fan culture surrounding it. This is surprising, considering it has only been in existence for less than 50 years, a short space of time compared to most popular games and less than many popular film and television franchises. But, since *D&D* is less of a story in and of itself and more of a springboard for individual groups to create their own stories, this means that the number of opaque slang, notorious fan stories, inside jokes, and recurring memes is staggering. Of course, understanding all of this ephemera is not essential to enjoying yourself at the table, but it is still useful to have at least a baseline understanding of where the game of *Dungeon & Dragons* came from and how it has not just shaped popular culture, but given rise to a whole new form of media.

Humble Beginnings

It's a bit difficult to pinpoint the moment at which *Dungeons & Dragons* truly came into being. This is mainly because it was never intended to be its own game at all. The original version of *D&D* came about as a combination of two different supplements to an existing miniature wargame.

This type of game had been in existence since the late 18th century and involved simulating historical battles using miniature soldiers on a map, originally as a means of training army officers in battlefield tactics, though they quickly developed into a form of recreation for civilians as well. In 1967, a designer by the name of Henry Bodenstedt published a wargame called Siege of Bodenburg, which, in contrast to most of the popular titles in the genre at the time, was meant to simulate the military conflicts of the Medieval Era, rather than the Napoleonic Wars, which were the subject of most popular wargames.

A year later, E. Gary Gygax, a wargame enthusiast discovered Siege of Bodenburg at a gaming convention in his hometown of Lake Geneva, Wisconsin. Excited by the idea of a medieval wargame but taking issue with some of Bodenstedt's design decisions, Gygax and his friend Jeff Perren, who owned the local game shop, decided to develop their own take on the concept, which they called *Chainmail*. The rules for *Chainmail* were first published in 1971 in the form of a 14-page pamphlet printed by Guidon Games. Alongside this booklet was a supplement authored by Gygax that included additional rules to incorporate elements of the pulp fantasy novels that he and many of his social circle had grown up reading: *Conan the Barbarian*, *Three Hearts and Three Lions*, Michael Moorcock's *Elric* series, and, of course, *The Lord of the Rings*.

Chainmail and its fantasy supplement were a modest hit, eventually falling into the hands of Dave Arneson, another wargamer living in Saint Paul, Minnesota. Arneson and his gaming group combined *Chainmail* with a military strategy game they enjoyed called *Braunstein*, which involved players not only controlling armies but also individual civilians in a small German town during the Napoleonic Wars. They liked the idea of incorporating non-combat actions into the simulation, but had been frustrated by the game's rather flimsy combat rules. The story goes that in the very first game of *Braunstein* they played, two of the players tried to get their civilian characters to duel one another, but were frustrated to discover that the rules did not account for this possibility. *Chainmail*, on the other hand, included rules for both mass and one-on-one combat, which made up for this deficiency.

As time went on, Arneson started incorporating ideas of his own as his group became more and more interested in playing as their individual characters instead of controlling large armies. Eventually, this frankensteined version of *Chainmail*, *Braunstein*, and Arneson's own contributions came to be called *Blackmoor*, named for the Barony of Blackmoor, which was the medieval fantasy realm he had created as a setting for the game, and the castle therein, whose extensive underground dungeons had been the main site of his group of players' adventures.

Arneson and Gygax were already loosely acquainted, having met through their mutual love of tabletop gaming, even collaborating in the past on previous Guidon Games projects. But, when Arneson approached Gygax and showed him how he had expanded *Chainmail*, the pair decided that this new game called for refinement and publication. Working out of Gygax's basement, Arneson, Gygax, and a group of other gamers including some of Gygax's children, playtested what they were then calling "the Fantasy Game." Eventually they settled on the name by which the game is still known today: *Dungeons & Dragons.*

Original Dungeons & Dragons

The original 1974 edition of *Dungeons & Dragons* was a set of three 30-40 page paperback booklets that were sold as a boxed set in hobby stores, bearing the name of Arneson and Gygax's new company: Tactical Rules Systems or TSR. The suggested retail price of this set was $10, an astronomical sum in those days for something as frivolous as a game. But, in defiance of what many early detractors predicted, it was this high price tag that caused many people frequenting these specialty hobby shops to pick *D&D* up. What kind of game could possibly warrant such a high cost?

The game was undeniably a hit, selling 1,000 copies in its first year and 3,000 the year after that. It was wholly unlike any other game on the market, injecting narrative and roleplay into the familiar wargaming framework. However, despite its success and the groundbreaking nature of this early version of the game, it's almost comical to look at now. The booklets were produced on a miniscule budget, with much of the artwork contributed by friends and family who would work for cheap. The result is that most of the illustrations are barely above a kindergartener's doodle in terms of skill and detail. The formatting, likewise, leaves much to be desired. Gygax and Arneson were idiosyncratic in their writing style and organization of rules and ideas, so looking for information about a specific aspect of the game in these booklets could be a frustrating and difficult affair.

Perhaps the most frustrating aspect of it was that, underneath it all, the 1974 *Dungeons & Dragons* was still primarily designed as an add-on for *Chainmail*, a game which it quickly eclipsed in popularity. This meant that, if you didn't own a copy of *Chainmail*, in order to run a game of *Dungeons & Dragons* involved a lot of inventing your own rules to fill in the gaps. To their credit, Gygax and Arneson recognized this shortcoming fairly quickly and, as more and more people began picking up *D&D* who had never even heard of *Chainmail*, they continued publishing supplementary booklets to the initial three, adding more rules and filling in some of the holes so that *Chainmail* was no longer necessary to get the complete game experience. However, with the game experience spread out across so many products, it soon became clear that the game needed to be collected in a form that would be easier for players to reference and simpler for shops to market to interested customers.

Basic and Advanced

Another concern that TSR set out to address when compiling and revising the rules for the new and improved *Dungeons & Dragons*, which would come to market in 1977, was the increased diversity in the player base. The original run of booklets had been designed for people who were already well-versed in the trappings of tabletop wargaming and, as such, used a great deal of jargon and complicated rules systems that were hard to parse for outsiders. But *D&D*'s popularity had expanded by this point to include people whose tabletop gaming experience didn't extend much beyond chess, checkers, and Monopoly. These new players were intrigued by the hype surrounding this new game, but were often frustrated by the density of the rules.

In order to cater both to veterans and new gamers, Gygax and company decided to split *Dungeons & Dragons* into two separate product lines. *Advanced Dungeons & Dragons* would be an elaboration on the rules that had been laid out in the original booklets, with everything that players and Dungeon Masters needed to know from a rules standpoint contained within three hardcover rulebooks. New versions of these same rule books have subsequently been published with every new edition of the game, bearing the same titles: *The Player's Handbook*, *The Dungeon Master's Guide*, and *The Monster Manual*.

Meanwhile, *Basic Dungeons & Dragons*, the product line meant as an entree for tabletop novices, was published primarily in the form of boxed sets that contained not only the rulebook, but also a set of dice and other supplementary materials. These boxes were designed to be stocked in toy stores, not just hobby shops, and the rule books they contained included a streamlined version of the game that was easier to approach for someone who had never played a wargame.

Despite the intent being for *Basic Dungeons & Dragons* to serve as a tool to hook new players who would then "graduate" to *Advanced D&D*, the original box set ended up being a consistent top-seller for TSR. This was helped by the fact that, while *Basic D&D* was playable right out of the box when it hit the shelf in 1977, the three core rulebooks needed to play *Advanced D&D* each took a year to publish. This meant that, if you wanted to play the more complex version of the game and didn't want to deal with trying to jury rig the 1977 *Monster Manual* with the old material from the paperback pamphlets, you would have to wait until 1979 for all of the new rulebooks to be released so that you could finally run the game in its most fully-realized form.

The result is that these two versions of the game experienced a parallel, divergent evolution. Rather than moving onto the *Advanced* product line, there was greater player demand for elaborations on the *Basic* rules, which led to a revised version of the boxed set in 1981, followed by additional boxes that added rules for increasingly high level play with each release. These were known as the *Expert*, *Companion*, *Master*, and *Immortals* sets. If you ever hear an older player fondly reminisce about "the red and black boxes" or

"BECMI," this is what they are referring to. For many children of the 80s, the all-in-one boxed sets of *Basic Dungeons & Dragons* were the start of a lifelong love of tabletop roleplaying games. However, many of these children's parents had taken notice of how devoted their kids had become to their new hobby and, when they thumbed through the rulebooks for themselves, many of them were none too pleased with what they found inside.

The Satanic Panic

The 1980s were a time of great moral panic across the United States and, other than rock and roll, *Dungeons & Dragons* was considered the greatest corruptor of America's youth. There were several reasons that *D&D* and the wider ecosystem of role-playing games that had sprung up around it gained this notoriety. Perhaps the biggest of these was the suicide of Irving Pulling, a young man who struggled with depression and anxiety and who also happened to be an active tabletop RPG player. In her grief over his death, his mother Patricia Pulling latched onto these two, probably unrelated, facts about her son and concluded that he had killed himself as a result of his involvement in *Dungeons & Dragons*, which had loosened his grip on reality.

Drawing on this belief and other cases where teenagers and young adults who happened to be a part of the hobby died or disappeared under mysterious circumstances, Patricia Pulling formed a parents organization called Bothered About Dungeons A Dragons, or BADD. BADD published pamphlets decrying the evils of roleplaying games and Patricia appeared frequently in the media discussing how *D&D* used "demonology, witchcraft, voodoo, murder, rape, blasphemy, suicide, assassination, insanity, sex perversion, homosexuality, prostitution, satanic type rituals, gambling, barbarism, cannibalism, sadism, desecration, demon summoning, necromantics, divination and other teachings" to corrupt impressionable youth and draw them into Satan's web.

To anyone who took the time to actually understand *Dungeons & Dragons*, this "Satanic Panic" was patently ridiculous. While demons and devils have been a fixture of *D&D* since the original edition, they have always been presented as enemies to defeat, not tempters to follow. This uproar was especially bewildering to Gary Gygax, who was himself a lifelong Jehovah's Witness and was known to go door to door handing out pamphlets for the church at various points in his life. Yet now he found himself dealing with threatening phone calls at TSR's offices and ended up having to hire a bodyguard because of the very real fear that one of these hysterical moral crusaders would try to attack him.

The silver lining in all of this was that, much like heavy metal music, the notoriety *Dungeons & Dragons* had gained from the Satanic Panic translated into bigger sales than ever before. This culminated in TSR

releasing a new edition of the *Advanced Dungeons &
Dragons* product line starting in 1989 that, in an
attempt to duck some of the heat from the moral
crusaders, excised a few of the more questionable
elements from the previous edition of the game.
Nevertheless, *Advanced Dungeons & Dragons Second
Edition* would prove to be one of the most popular
versions of *D&D* ever released. However, by this point,
TSR had expanded far beyond any of the founders'
wildest dreams and it wouldn't be too long before
they'd find their faculties extended beyond what they
were capable of handling.

The Downfall of TSR

What ultimately killed TSR was overzealousness. The
runaway success of the second edition of *Advanced
D&D* led to the publishing of a glut of supplements and
tie-in products. This rising tide also lifted the basic
version of the game as well and soon TSR found itself
with an unsustainable number of different product
lines, including not just the two versions of *Dungeons
& Dragons* and a handful of other roleplaying games,
but also many books and boxsets for D&D games
themed around different settings. These included Dark
Sun, a post-apocalyptic version of the game
reminiscent of *Mad Max* meets *Conan the Barbarian*,
Ravenloft, set in a world inspired by gothic horror
literature, and Spelljammer, which took players on

adventures through the stars, courtesy of Jules Verne-esque space vessels.

The problem was that, though there were more people playing *Dungeons & Dragons* as a whole than ever before, most of these individual projects did not generate enough sales to make up for the cost in developing and printing them. Gygax had also become obsessed with creating more and more *D&D* tie-in merchandise, which was expensive to produce and generally sold quite poorly. He also became obsessed with selling the idea of a movie based on the game to Hollywood. This was an obsession that some of the cooler heads at TSR eventually realized they could use to keep him in California on the company dime, a small price to pay to keep his frivolous impulses from doing further damage to his Lake Geneva-based company's rapidly deteriorating finances.

The writing was on the walls, though. By 1997, TSR teetered on the brink of bankruptcy with the future of *Dungeons & Dragons* hanging in the balance. Thankfully, as has happened in countless *D&D* games, when things looked bleak, a powerful wizard swooped in and saved the day.

Wizards of the Coast

In 1997, Wizards of the Coast was, in many ways, what TSR had been when it burst onto the scene in the mid

70s. The company had introduced the concept of the collectible trading card game with the release of *Magic: The Gathering* in 1993 and had become fabulously successful as a result. Recognizing the value of the *Dungeons & Dragons* brand, the Seattle-based company purchased TSR, saving them from bankruptcy, and set to work trimming the fat from *D&D* from a business standpoint. This included jettisoning many of the ancillary products to focus on the core game and the medieval fantasy it was best known for.

They also recognized that maintaining two separate versions of the same game had long since ceased making sense from either a business or a player experience standpoint. Consequently, when Wizards of the Coast released the third edition of *Dungeons & Dragons* in 2000, it was as a single, unified system, ending the Basic/Advanced divide that had been in place for over 20 years.

This new edition was a radical departure from what had come before and, as a result, it initially was met with skepticism by long-time players. The rules were at once more thoughtfully designed and far more complex than previous editions and, despite its long development cycle, there were a number of fundamental flaws with the core rules of the new "d20 System" that had been created for the new version of the game. As a result, in 2003, a soft reboot of the game, dubbed "3.5," was released to plug these holes.

Despite coming with a significantly steeper learning curve than any previous iteration of *Dungeons & Dragons*, this version would grow to a cherished place in the fanbase. It was praised for putting more power in the hands of the players, allowing for greater character customization and rules that gave them a fairer shake at surviving their first foray into a dungeon than ever before. This, combined with the wealth of material available to players, thanks to the decision to make the fundamental rules of the system an open document that other companies could use to create *D&D*-compatible books of their own, made the game a hit. However, this over-abundance of material of variable quality, some of it even published by Wizards of the Coast, quickly made the third edition a bloated, unbalanced mess of a game. This led the powers-that-be to try and streamline the game and, after only five years, retire the flawed-but-beloved edition in favor of something radically new.

The Wilderness Years of Fourth Edition

In 2005, Wizards of the Coast released *Dungeons & Dragons: Fourth Edition*. This new version of the game took cues from the emerging popularity of massively multiplayer online games like *World of Warcraft*, which had, themselves, taken immense inspiration from *Dungeons & Dragons*. It was more streamlined, its rules easier to follow, and its system optimized to balance the power of the various character classes. In light of how over-complicated the last edition had been, it stood to reason, the designers thought, that players would welcome a simpler version of the game that kept its player-focus while making it less of a headache to play. Instead, they started leaving the game in droves.

Despite how clunky it was, the third edition still felt like *Dungeons & Dragons* to long-time players. This new version felt like a whole new game and one that jettisoned a lot of what they had liked and replaced it with rules that seemed tailored to try to compete with video games. As a result, many of these dissatisfied players stopped playing *D&D* altogether, instead picking up other roleplaying games. One massive benefactor of this exodus was a gaming company named Paizo, who had published a lot of well-regarded material under the open gaming license that Wizards of the Coast had created for the third edition. They realized that, though Wizards of the Coast was no longer publishing third edition material, nothing in the license prevented them from continuing to do so. So, in 2009, they released their own fantasy RPG, *Pathfinder*, based on *D&D 3.5* and, as such, compatible with everything that had been released for that edition.

In the minds of many players, *Pathfinder*, not *D&D Fourth Edition*, was the true heir to Arneson and Gygax's legacy. This spelled trouble for the team at Wizards of the Coast who, despite a valiant effort to expand their game to appeal to the masses, ultimately were forced to admit that they'd diverged too far from the formula and a course correction was needed.

The D&D Renaissance

Playtesting for the fifth edition, originally called *D&D Next*, began in 2012. From the beginning, there was a strong emphasis from the development team on getting player input. They wanted to find where they went wrong with the fourth edition so that they could win back some of the player base that had left for *Pathfinder* and other competing games while still making a version of the game that was less convoluted than the third. After two years, on the 40th anniversary of the release of the original three pamphlets, *Dungeons & Dragons: Fifth Edition* was released to near immediate acclaim.

It is no exaggeration to say that we are living in something of a renaissance for *Dungeons & Dragons* and roleplaying games in general. The ease of play of fifth edition has coincided with a wellspring of media that promotes the game to new audiences. You yourself may have first gotten interested in the game via a podcast or video stream showcasing charismatic people playing *Dungeons & Dragons* together. This, perhaps more than any innovation in game design, has led to the skyrocketing popularity the game has enjoyed over the past eight years.

Ultimately, the reason that these showcases have been so effective is that they have dispelled a lot of the negative stereotypes that have long persisted regarding what *Dungeons & Dragons* is and why people enjoy playing it. It's not just a game about rolling dice and moving tiny figurines around on a grid. It's a social activity with much the same vibe as a poker night. It's also a unique opportunity to experience a story in which you are both the audience and a main character. Finally, it's an opportunity to experiment with what it's like to be someone else.

Chapter 2: Playing Dungeons & Dragons

Now that we've covered the appeal of *Dungeons & Dragons* and also given you a survey of the game's history, let's get down to what you came here for: how do you play the game?

Though the *Player's Handbook* is, ultimately, the definitive guide on this subject, this chapter is meant to be a streamlined reference point for the most basic facts about how the game works. This will introduce you to important concepts that will give you a headstart if and when you read the official rules. It will also give you a foundational understanding of the rules that will help you understand some of the higher-level concepts we will talk about in subsequent chapters.

Roles at the Table

One of the things that makes a tabletop RPG unlike most other types of games is that it is an asymmetrical experience for the people playing it. The majority of players at the table control fantasy heroes working together to achieve a common goal. There are usually four or five of these players, though the game can still work with as few as one or as many as ten, if everyone involved is experienced and mature enough.

The important thing is that one player acts as the Dungeon Master. They are the referee and also the chief storyteller. They control all aspects of the world that the other players interact with and prepare the narrative that the game session follows. If *The Lord of the Rings* were a game of *D&D*, the player characters might be Frodo, Gandalf, and Aragorn, but the DM would be J.R.R. Tolkein.

Game Equipment

Though *Dungeons & Dragons* is not a board game per se, there are a number of materials that can enhance the experience. Ultimately, though, no piece of equipment is 100% essential. There are even accounts of prison inmates playing *D&D* who found ways to eliminate even the need for dice, which were not allowed in the cell block because of rules against gambling. However, there are materials that are ubiquitous or at least commonly found at your average *D&D* table.

Rulebooks

As of this writing, there are more than 30 official books in print by Wizards of the Coast for the *Dungeons & Dragons: Fifth Edition* ruleset. Since the current edition, like the third edition, operates on an open license, there are also countless third-party supplements that may also be in use at any given table. The good news is that, especially as a new player, you will probably not be expected to invest in any of them up-front. Each of these books typically retails for $30-50, so most players and Dungeon Masters will understand if you're not ready to put down that kind of money before you're sure that this is a hobby you want to pursue long-term.

If, however, you catch the bug after your first few sessions, especially if you decide you want to try your hand at DMing, you'll have to pick up at least a few rulebooks. We'll go into further detail about the major types of rulebooks and which ones you'll need in the next chapter. For now, suffice to say that, if you plan on becoming a regular player, at some point you're going to have to buy your own copy of the *Player's Handbook* at the very least. Once you're no longer a beginner, constantly having to borrow from other group members is just bad form.

Character Sheets

A character sheet is, simply put, a piece of paper that summarizes what your character can do. Back in the 70s, this was usually just a sheet of notebook paper. Now, though you can of course still take the old-school approach, it's more common to use the official template that you can download for free online. If you own a copy of the *Player's Handbook*, there is also a blank character sheet in the back that you can photocopy whenever you make a new character.

It also bears mentioning that there are a number of online applications that can act as a digital character sheet, automating a lot of the math and streamlining the choices that you inevitably have to make when building a new character. The most well known of these is DnD Beyond, a service which licenses all of the official rulebooks from Wizards of the Coast, though accessing anything other than the free Basic Rules requires an additional purchase. My advice is that, once you are no longer a novice, if such an aid appeals to you, then by all means, go for it. But, when making your first character, filling out the sheet by hand acts as a valuable primer on the rules and will make you less flustered when you sit down to play. For what it's worth, despite now being extremely seasoned as both a player and Dungeon Master for this edition of *Dungeons & Dragons* and being fairly tech-savvy, I still fill out all of my character sheets by hand.

Dice

Perhaps the most iconic aspect of *D&D* is the many polyhedral dice that are used to play. One of the first lessons that a new player learns is differentiating the dice types from one another, since most other dice games only involve the standard, six-sided variety. In RPGs, the type of dice called for for any given roll is referred to by the letter "d" (for "die") followed by a number indicating the number of faces. So, for example, the common, cube-shaped die that you are familiar with is called a d6. If you are required to roll multiple dice of the same type, that is indicated by the number of dice in front of the "d." For example, the damage caused by a strike with a greatsword is 2d6, or two rolls of six-sided die. A standard set of RPG dice will consist of, at a bare minimum, seven dice: a d20, a d12, two d10s, a d8, a d6, and a d4.

The d20 is, hands down, the most important die in the set for *Dungeons & Dragons*. It is easily the die you will roll most often, as the entire game system is built around rolling d20s to determine if your character succeeds or fails at the tasks they attempt, be that picking the lock on a treasure chest or hitting an enemy with an attack. Because of this, a seasoned player usually has more d20s in their dice collection than any other die. RPG players are a superstitious lot and, if one d20 isn't rolling well for you on a given night, it gives you a sense of comfort and control to be able to swap in a new one in the hopes that it will treat you better. In fact, for many players, testing which of their d20s are "hot" with a few practice rolls is an important part of their pregame ritual. You can distinguish it because, of the "standard" RPG dice, it is the one that is closest to a sphere.

The d20 is easiest to confuse with the d12. The easiest way to avoid making that mistake without having to count all of the sides is that a d20 has triangular faces while a d12's faces are shaped like pentagons. The d12 is not especially commonly used in *Dungeons & Dragons*. Some people call it the "Barbarian's die" partially because characters of the Barbarian class will base their maximum number of hit points, the measure of their character's health and ability to take damage, off of the d12. The other reason for the nickname is that it is also the die you roll to determine how much damage you do if you successfully hit an enemy with a greataxe, a weapon most commonly wielded by Barbarians.

D10s can be distinguished by the unusual and irregular shape of their faces. If you're a geometry nerd, you'll note that they are the only dice that are not "Platonic solids," which is also why the modern d10 wasn't invented until 1980, while all of the other standard RPG dice have ancestors that date back millenia. Before then, to fulfill the function of a d10, gamers would use special d20s numbered 1-10 twice. D10s have a number of different uses in *Dungeons & Dragons*. Several weapons and spells use them to determine damage in the event of a successful attack.

They are also used to determine hit points for hearty characters like those of the Paladin, Fighter, and Ranger classes. Their most unique function, and the reason a set usually contains two of them, is for generating numbers between one and 100, a roll that can be notated or referred to as "d100," "d%," or "percentile dice." This is not as commonly called for in *Dungeons & Dragons* as it is in some other systems (*Call of Cthulhu*, for instance, uses this in similar manner to how *D&D* uses d20 rolls), but your DM might still call for it to determine certain, usually random effects.

Reading the result of this roll can be tricky to learn, but it's actually relatively simple once you understand how d10s are numbered. If you're looking at two d10s from the same set, one will be numbered 1-9 with the tenth side labeled "0." It is important to understand that the "0" is actually read as a result of ten when this die is rolled individually. You can't roll a zero on a d10, just like you can't roll a zero on any other die. The reason it's numbered that way is to cut down on confusion when rolled with the other d10 in the set, which is numbered by tens 10-90 with "00" on the tenth side. When rolling percentile dice, it's simply a matter of adding the results of the two dice, reading the single "0" as a "0," not "10." If both zeroes come up, that is considered a result of 100. Finally, if you are rolling using two ordinary d10s, you simply designate one of them to be the tens place and the other to be the ones place, following the same rule of double zeroes being 100.

The d8, which some describe as "diamond-shaped," is perhaps the most commonly used die in the game. Seven out of the 12 character classes detailed in the *Player's Handbook* generate their maximum hit points using it and it is also used to determine damage for popular weapons like rapiers and longswords. It is also the second most often-used die for spell damage.

The most common die for spell damage is the familiar d6. Many of the game's most popular spells deal damage based on various numbers of d6. It is also used for determining weapon damage for things like shortswords and spears, among others. Finally, classes gifted with access to powerful magical abilities, namely the Wizard and the Sorcerer, determine hit points using the d6, as the trade-off for access to this kind of arcane power is a frailer-than-average body.

This brings us to the d4. While daggers do damage measured by the roll of 1d4 and each of the three bursts of energy generated by the Magic Missile spell famously deals 1d4+1 force damage, the you'll most often roll a d4 if you have a member of the Cleric class in your group. This is because Clerics have access to a number of spells that bolster their allies' capabilities via the addition of 1d4 to various types of d20 rolls, as well as others that can weaken their enemies by forcing them to subtract 1d4 from their d20 rolls in a similar way.

This is a quick overview of the uses for each die. Generally speaking, as a brand new player, you probably don't need to get your own dice if you're not ready to commit. If your DM is like me, they probably have a special stock of dice that they loan out to new players who are trying the game for the first time. That said, a set of quality resin dice can usually be found for under $10, a significantly smaller investment than a rulebook, so you'd hardly be looked at askance if you were to grab a set of your own dice before your first game. If you don't, they'll probably be the first thing your group will expect you to get for yourself, so if you feel confident this isn't going to be a one-time thing, why not pull the trigger on buying your first set?

Maps and Miniatures

Strictly speaking, *Dungeons & Dragons* can be played purely using your imagination. If the Dungeon Master is gifted at describing situations and everyone is fully engaged with the story, the entire game can be played in the style of "theater of the mind," the term that has evolved over the years to describe this kind of playing style. However, particularly in combat scenarios, most gaming groups find it more convenient to have a visual aid for where their characters are relative to each other, their enemies, and the environment. This allows them to devote less concentration to maintaining a clear mental picture and instead spend that mental energy on carefully considering their next move. It also makes some spells and abilities a bit easier to use in a way that feels objective and fair, since it gives the group a way to accurately measure things like distance and areas of effect.

How sophisticated this representation is can vary wildly from table to table. Speaking from personal experience, I've had wonderful results using a simple dry-erase mat with a grid of one-inch squares and some cheap wooden nickels I bought at a craft store. But, depending on budget and available prep time, these "battle maps" can consist of intricate sculpted terrain and meticulously hand-painted custom mini-figurines to represent each character, PC and enemy alike, creating an immersive visual experience akin to a museum diorama. Most *D&D* tables fall somewhere in between these two extremes.

This is advanced-level stuff, though, and nothing that you need to get overly concerned about as a newcomer. In Chapter 5, which is all about combat, we'll talk a little bit more in-depth about how these visual aids work in practice, but for now it's enough to know that they exist and are another common piece of *D&D* accoutrement that can greatly enhance the game experience.

Basic Game Mechanics: The Three Main Types of Dice Rolls

"This is all well and good," you might be thinking, "But how do I actually play the game?" Well, we're going to take a deep dive into the particulars in the next three chapters, but for now, it's best to start by going over the three main types of dice rolls that you'll be asked to make as a player. In many ways, these form the backbone of the fifth edition's game system: Skill checks, attack rolls, and saving throws.

Skill Checks

A skill check is a roll of a d20 to which you add a bonus (or penalty) determined by your character's statistics as well as their proficiency in certain specialized tasks. The DM will ask you to make a specific type of skill check when your character attempts to do something in the game world like pick a lock, break down a door, or recall information about a magical creature. The result of this roll is compared against a number determined in secret by the Dungeon Master based on how difficult the task you're trying to accomplish is. This is referred to as the check's Difficulty Class, or DC. If your result equals or exceeds the DC, you succeed at the task. If you fall short of it, you fail.

For example, let's say that you are trying to bribe a member of the local city watch to give you some information. The DM will ask you to make a Persuasion check, mentally setting the DC at 14. You roll your d20 and get a "10." You then look at your character sheet and see that Persuasion checks receive a bonus equal to your Charisma modifier, which is a +2, and that you are proficient in these checks, allowing you to add another +2 bonus for a total of +4. Adding this to the number on the die, you get a "14," meeting the Difficulty Class. The guard takes the coin and tells you the information you were looking for.

This might sound like a lot of steps to resolve a simple situation, but as part of the process of making your character, you'll already have filled out all of the bonuses that apply to each type of skill check on your character sheet, so referencing this information should be relatively quick once you get used to the layout of the sheet. We'll talk more about this process in Chapter 4, which is about building a character.

Attack Rolls

Attack rolls are most commonly called for in an active combat situation. Much like a skill check, you make an attack roll to see whether you are successful when you try to hit an enemy with a weapon or spell. The difference is that, unlike the DC of skill checks, which is determined by the DM, each creature or object in *Dungeons & Dragons* has a numerical measure of how hard they are to hit based on their equipment and natural resistance to damage. This number is called an Armor Class or AC. Much like with skill checks and DCs, the goal of an attack roll is to meet or exceed your target's AC. If you hit, you roll damage dice depending on the type of attack.

An important thing to note is that if the "20" face of your d20 comes up on an attack roll, that is what is known as a "natural 20" or "critical hit." When this happens, not only do you automatically hit your target, you also get to roll twice as many damage dice as normal, creating the opportunity to do massive amounts of damage. It is also worth noting that when the "1" face comes up, this "natural 1" is considered an automatic failure, though, at least according to the rules-as-written, no additional misfortune occurs. This is frequently ignored by many Dungeon Masters who like to inflict cruel and unusual punishments on their players when they roll poorly.

Saving Throws

In contrast to skill checks and attack rolls, saving throws are typically initiated by the actions of the DM, rather than player choice. These rolls are made to try to avoid damage and other adverse effects, hence the name saving throws. Like skill checks, success or failure on a saving throw is determined by measuring the result of the d20 roll against a Difficulty Class, though the DCs for things like spells cast by enemy combatants tend to be calculated with more exact formulas than the more free-wheeling DCs of many skill checks.

Like skill checks, saving throws are keyed to ability scores, with each character class granting a proficiency bonus to two of the six types of saves: one from the three more commonly called-for saves (Dexterity, Wisdom, and Constitution) and another from the three rarer saving throws (Strength, Charisma, and Intelligence). For any given saving throw the DM calls for, you roll the d20, add the relevant ability modifier and proficiency bonus, if applicable, and the DM compares it against the DC of the effect to determine what happens as a result.

All three of these types of rolls, skill checks, attack rolls, and saving throws, are subject to another core mechanic introduced in the newest edition of the game to simplify the system of finicky and heavily circumstantial bonuses that were common in the third and fourth editions. This mechanic is called Advantage/Disadvantage. Various abilities and circumstances can give you either Advantage or Disadvantage on a d20 roll. If you are granted Advantage, you get to roll your d20 twice (or just roll two dice at the same time) and take the higher of the two results. Conversely, if you are given Disadvantage, you must roll twice and take the lower result.

It is important to note that, regardless of how many circumstances are in your favor (or working against you, as the case may be), you can never roll more than two d20s as a result of this mechanic. Additionally, if you are in a situation where both Advantage and Disadvantage apply to the same roll, the two cancel each other out, no matter how many effects are granting Advantage or Disadvantage.

Chapter 3: Getting Started on Your Own

Since we've covered the barest of bare bones information that you need to know if asked to join someone else's table, I'd like to take a moment here to speak to special considerations that have to be made if you're trying to get into this hobby of your own volition and don't necessarily know anyone that plays, at least not well enough to ask them to run a game for you. All of the information from the previous chapter still applies, of course, but being in this situation means that there are some additional considerations and obstacles that need to be surmounted before you can get to the fun of actually playing the game.

Finding a Group (Or Starting One Yourself)

If you don't have an experienced friend who already has an established group that you can slot into, finding a gaming group can be a daunting prospect. Starting any new hobby can be scary and finding yourself at a toxic table as a beginner has turned many would-be adventurers off of tabletop gaming completely. That said, thanks to *Dungeons & Dragons'* greater-than-ever popularity, it is easier than ever before to either find or make a quality group for your first experience.

First and most obviously, talk to your existing social circle. While you may not know anyone that plays, you may have enough friends with an interest in or at least curiosity about the game to be willing to give it a try. It's undeniably more work to learn the ropes when even the DM is new to this, but it can also be incredibly liberating not to feel judged for your inexperience. If everyone is learning together, then no one has any cause to feel embarrassed for making a mistake or not knowing how a spell or other game mechanic works. And, who knows, maybe one of your friends knows someone with DMing experience that they can hook you up with or call in to run the session for your group.

If this isn't an option for you, then your next best avenue is to see if there is a gaming hobby shop in your area that deals in tabletop RPG books and materials. Within the community, these kinds of businesses are referred to as FLGSs, which stands for "Friendly Local Game Stores." These make for good places to meet people with an interest in *Dungeons & Dragons* and other roleplaying games; many of them even have communal bulletin boards where people advertise that they are looking for players or game masters. Many of them also offer organized play events, like the official Wizards of the Coast-sponsored Adventurers' League. These events, usually held on a weekly or biweekly basis, offer a polished play experience with games catering to all skill levels run by experienced Dungeon Masters, often employees or trusted regulars of the shop. Since the entire reason these events exist is to attract new players to the hobby and, by extension, new customers to the business, Adventurers' League events can be an easy entry point into *Dungeons & Dragons.*

Finally, if you live in a remote area with no FLGS and you can't find enough people in your social circle to put together a group of newbies, there is always the internet. The fifth edition of the game has benefited greatly from the advances in digital technology that have been made over the past decade, including online forums like Reddit, which hosts a sizeable community of tabletop gamers, as well as virtual tabletop applications, sites that are designed to allow a GM to run their games for players all over the world. Many of these forums and applications have a section where players and DMs can find one another. Simply be on the lookout for the acronym "LFG," community slang for "looking for group," and see if anything catches your eye. Better yet, make a post yourself. Explain that you're new and trying to learn the ropes and, with any luck, you'll find a DM who will be willing to take you under their wing.

If, however, you find yourself putting together your own group from the ground up, then you will have to do a little bit of shopping to get started. Thankfully, as we discussed in the last chapter, there are very few things that are absolutely essential to get started in *Dungeons & Dragons*, even if you're starting from square one.

The Rules

Ultimately, all you really need for a game of *Dungeons & Dragons* is some friends, some dice, and a point of reference for the rules of the game. Some other things are nice and make things easier, but that's really all that is absolutely necessary. Dice, as we've covered, are relatively cheap and increasingly easier to come by. What can be intimidating is picking out which rulebooks you need when just starting out. In truth, there are actually a number of options open to you, depending on how invested you want to get out of the gate and how much work whoever has agreed to DM for your group is willing to put in as far as creating their own story.

The Basic Rules

The barest of the bare-bones options is the Basic Rules. This is a free, stripped down version of the fifth edition game system that is freely available in PDF form from Wizards of the Coast. This contains information on all of the major game systems as well as information on building characters of a limited number of classes and subclasses with a likewise limited spell selection. If you are looking for something simple and straightforward, this is for you.

The trade-off here is that, while the basic rules are good for players, they don't have much for the Dungeon Master beyond the simplest advice, a few stat blocks, and magic item descriptions. There is no pre-written adventure in the Basic Rules and making your own can be difficult if you've never experienced *Dungeons & Dragons* before. Ultimately, though, beggars can't really be choosers when you're talking about a free product.

Box Sets

Harkening back to the days of BECMI, the next step up from the Basic Rules are the box sets. There are a number of these offerings currently in print from Wizards of the Coast, the two most prominent being titled the *Starter Set* and the *Essentials Kit*. Both sets contain a printed copy of the Basic Rules document, as well as character sheets, dice, and a pre-written adventure. The main difference between the two, other than which adventure is included in the box, is that the *Starter Set* contains pre-made character sheets, whereas the *Essentials Kit* has, as part of its rulebook, instructions on how to make a character step-by-step.

You'll have to decide which of these options is more appealing to you.

I recommend this as your starting point if you're willing to spend some money, but aren't sure yet whether this hobby is going to be an ongoing pursuit for you, so you aren't ready to commit to buying the full rulebooks yet. This is mainly because of the adventures they contain. Both *The Lost Mines of Phandelver*, which comes with the *Starter Set*, and *The Dragon of Icespire Peak*, which is the centerpiece of the *Essentials Kit*, are quality introductory adventures for both new players and new Dungeon Masters. If you've never played *D&D* before and are trying to DM right out of the gate, you're going to have enough on your plate without also trying to come up with a compelling story. These boxsets take care of that part of your job for you so that you can focus on learning how to prep and run the game.

There are other boxed sets besides these two, mostly co-branded products that Wizards of the Coast has put out as tie-ins with popular television shows that have featured *Dungeons & Dragons*. As of this writing, the two most prominent and popular of these have been co-branded with *Stranger Things* and *Rick and Morty*, of which I've only played the latter. It was certainly a lot of fun and a nice change of pace for the group I played it with, but, while it does an adequate job of introducing the rules and concept of the game, it doesn't give you that classic *D&D* experience and atmosphere, for obvious reasons. Overall, I'd recommend you stick to two "classic" box sets unless you feel very strongly about wanting the slightly off-center vibe of learning the game with the unconventional flavor that these tie-in products bring.

The Core Rulebooks

Of course, for many people, anything worth trying is worth trying with all of the bells and whistles. The fact that the core rulebooks for fifth edition are available at a wide variety of retailers, often at discounted prices, means that it may not be too much of a monetary investment to start off with a more complete set of player options and DM information than is available in the Basic Rules or one of the boxsets.

The core rules for the fifth edition of *Dungeons & Dragons* are spread across three books, bearing the same names the core rulebooks have used since first edition *Advanced Dungeons & Dragons*: *The Player's Handbook*, *The Monster Manual*, and *The Dungeon Master's Guide*. As you may have intimated, the *Player's Handbook* is the most vital of these and the only one that a non-DM really needs to read. It contains all that you need to know about the way the game operates and, perhaps most importantly, information on how to make a character using any of the game's core character classes, with several subclass options for each.

The DM, though, should also have a copy of the *Dungeon Master's Guide* and especially the *Monster Manual*. Despite the name, the *Dungeon Master's Guide*, while useful, is essentially an elaboration on the *Player's Handbook* sprinkled with some useful tidbits and tips. It's certainly useful and deserving of its place in the "core three," but easily the least useful of the group. The *Monster Manual*, on the other hand, is a treasure trove of statblocks and lore on various creatures that a DM can use to build combat encounters and even use as inspiration for whole narratives. This is important to note, since none of these three core books contains a prewritten adventure, so if you're taking this route, your DM will have to either come up with their own ideas or spring for a module to run on top of these three rulebooks.

Though there is certainly no need to get any more than these three to start, in order to demystify the shelf of *D&D* books at Barnes and Noble or your FLGS, let's take a moment to talk about what all of those other books are and what they are for. That way, once you've gotten further into the hobby, you'll be able to make an educated decision about what, if anything, to get next.

Rules Expansions

The more common of these official non-core supplement books can be considered rules expansions. Think of these like expansion packs for a video game.

They can provide both players and Dungeon Masters with new content to bring spice to their games. The most popular of these rulebooks either center around providing new character creation options for the players or expanding on the menagerie of available monsters that the DM can use to challenge the party. Though there are many examples of both put out by various publishers, the official books released by Wizards of the Coast whose are generally accepted by most if not all Dungeon Masters are, for player options, *Xanathar's Guide to Everything* and *Tasha's Cauldron of Everything* and, for new creatures, *Volo's Guide to Monsters* and *Mordenkainen's Tome of Foes*.

The other major type of expansion book is called a campaign setting. These books often contain content for both DMs and players. Their main point is introducing a new fictional world in which the Dungeon Master can set their games, each of which has its own themes and flavors. The official campaign settings published for Wizards of the Coast are *Eberron: Rising from the Last War*, my personal favorite, which combines classic *D&D* adventuring with a 1940s pulp noir vibe and elements of steampunk; *Van Richten's Guide to Ravenloft*, an update on the gothic horror setting that dates back to the second addition; *The Explorer's Guide to Wildmount*, a collaboration with the popular *D&D* stream Critical Role detailing the Eastern European-inspired setting of their second long-term campaign; and, finally, Wizards of the Coast's own internal tie-in settings with *Magic: The Gathering*: the magitechheavy *Guildmaster's Guide to Ravnica,* the Greek-inspired *Mythic Odysseys of Theros,* and the Harry Potter-esque *Strixhaven: Curriculum of Chaos.*

Generally speaking, you can get by perfectly fine without one of these campaign guides. Any major new character options with applicability outside of the setting that introduced them tend to eventually get republished in future, non-setting books. The only reason to get one is if you are a Dungeon Master interested in the setting and think that you might want to run a game set in its world or pull elements of it to use in your own world. They can be a fun source of ideas, but, generally speaking, they are the least useful of the expansion books.

Adventure Modules

The main reason that there are so many books in print for the current edition of *Dungeons & Dragons* is that every year since the debut of fifth edition, Wizards of the Coast has issued at least one and usually two or more hardcover books containing a prewritten adventure either designed to form the basis of a long-term campaign, or else consisting of a number of shorter stories designed to be played in 1-3 sessions. If you've decided to jump in with both feet on getting the core rulebooks, I'd also highly recommend that the DM for your group also pick up one of these. The longer modules might be a bit intense to jump into right away for a new group, especially since the fact that they're meant to play out over the course of dozens of gaming sessions means that you probably won't get a satisfying experience your first time out of the gate. However, speaking from experience, the adventures from the anthology books make a great introduction for both new players and new Dungeon Masters. Each of these has a specific theme connecting the stories, so, if you want to keep going after you finish the first adventure in the anthology, it's pretty simple to segue into the next one.

But regardless of what your first adventure is, if you're a player, your first hurdle to overcome is building your first *D&D* character. This can be a confusing process for newcomers, not helped by the rather obtuse way that the *Player's Handbook* lays this out. So, our next chapter is going to break this process down in an easy to understand manner so that you can easily pull the information that you need from the official rules without having to spend time reading through the entire character creation portion of the *Player's Handbook*.

Chapter 4: Building a Character

Building your first character can act as a good introduction to the basic rules of *D&D*, since so much of the information that you fill in on your character sheet has to do with the way your specific character will interact with those rules. It also can be a way to get excited for the game. There's an undeniable thrill to learning about all of the cool stuff that you'll be able to do. I can distinctly remember, for instance, the first time I built a Monk fantasizing about the day that I'd get to use my character's ability to catch an arrow and throw it back at the person that fired it.

Making a character, at least from a mechanical standpoint, consists of three major choices: Background, which represents what your character had been up to before becoming an adventurer; Race, which is what species your character comes from; and Class, which describes the fantasy archetype that your character embodies. Each of these decisions will give you access to skills and abilities that, taken together, will turn your character sheet into a comprehensive picture of what your character can do and also point you towards a deeper understanding of their personality.

So as not to devalue the information contained in the *Player's Handbook,* as well as avoid plagiarizing the official rules, we'll be discussing your options here in broad terms, rather than getting in-depth on analyzing the mechanical implications of them. You should use this chapter as a survey of the options available to you so that, when you see something that sounds cool to you, you know what part of the *Player's Handbook* to look at to get the information about what to write down on your character sheet.

Background

Backgrounds are the simplest aspect of the character creation process. Each option gives you a package of skill, tool, or language proficiencies as well as some starting equipment. They can also play into fifth edition *D&D*'s "Trait/Ideal/Bond/Flaw" system, which is less of a rule, but more of an exercise that the designers have introduced to get you thinking about how to roleplay your character in social situations by giving them a quirk, a personal code, a deeply important belief or life priority, and a flaw that can get them into trouble. Each background option in the *Player's Handbook* gives you some suggestions for each of these things that is in line with the lifestyle that a character may have lived before the decision to take up an adventuring life.

There are so many of these backgrounds and they are so simple and self-explanatory that it doesn't make sense to give a thorough run down of each of them here. My advice is to either think of where you envision your character coming from and scan the background options to find one that most closely matches that idea or else scan through the options and see which one catches your interest.

Race

The various fantasy races that populate the world of *Dungeons & Dragons* are the first set of character options presented in the *Player's Handbook*. Each race comes with a lot of flavorful lore that can inform how your character sees and relates to the world of the game. Your choice of race will also impact your stats, skills, and may even give you fun abilities like the ability to cast a few spells. Though this does create some synergies with the class options making some combinations slightly more powerful, the current edition has done a good job of making sure that each race/class combination is viable, so I would advise you to focus more on what kind of story you're looking to tell with this character instead of trying to find the best combination. *D&D* isn't a competitive game, after all. All of that said, let's take a brief look at the options presented to you by the *Player's Handbook*.

Dragonborn

The dragonborn are, to put it simply, the result of dragon experimentation on humanoids. These tall, bulk, bipedal lizards have some innate magical abilities, including an elemental breath weapon that they can use a limited number of times in combat, just like their draconic ancestors. Clannish and insular, Dragonborn are one of the more unusual races to see out in the world, so you should be prepared for your character to attract some strange looks as, to the average peasant that has never left the village they were born in, you might look more like a monster than a hero at first blush.

Dwarf

Dwarves are a staple of fantasy literature, due in part to their long history with *Dungeons & Dragons*. If you're a *Lord of the Rings* fan, you'll probably already have a good feel for what dwarves are like. Stocky, bearded, and possessed of a weakness for treasure, dwarves are a people with a rich culture of both craftsmanship and warfare. The stereotypical dwarf enjoys and appreciates blacksmithing, ale, stonework, and has a strong ethical center, usually with a focus on their clan and family. One of the more common races in *D&D*, dwarves are a good choice for players for whom the aesthetic and idiosyncrasies of this race are appealing and who are looking for a choice that gives them a clear idea of where they fit into the game world.

Elf

Like dwarves, elves have been part of *D&D* from the very beginning. Also like dwarves, they have strong and obvious roots in the works of J.R.R. Tolkein. Elves are ethereal, long-lived, and have a stereotype of being aloof and cold in demeanor because of these facts. When making an elf character, you have three distinct options in terms of subrace. Other races have subrace options, but few impact the abilities and general vibe of a character the way that these elf options do. You can be a high elf, with innate abilities in magic or a wood elf, with swift feet and an affinity for nature. These archetypes are probably familiar to you from classic works of fantasy. However, the third option is distinctly *D&D*: the dark elf, also called drow. These gray-skinned elves dwell deep underground, where they live in a corrupt, matriarchal society centered around the worship of the evil spider goddess Lolth. Creating a drow character can be an interesting opportunity to either play into or subvert this stereotype.

Gnomes

This is one of the quirkier races. Gnomes are small, cute, and possessed with boundless energy and a zest for life. Gnomes, like elves, are cousins of the fey and, as a result, have a great deal of natural curiosity and tend to throw themselves into things that interest them with reckless abandon. They also have an inclination towards tinkering and some gnomes can build barely-functional clockwork creations that are as ingenious as they are incredibly unstable. Clever and foolhardy, gnomes can be something of the "class clown" race. One thing's for sure, though: they're rarely boring.

Half-Elf

Half-elves are the result of interbreeding between elves and humans. As a result, they share both their elf side's aesthetic sensibilities and some of their natural resistance to magic, as well their human half's versatility and drive. This internal dichotomy can be an interesting dynamic to roleplay. Some half-elves have very little angst relating to their heritage while others feel perpetually out of place, being neither fully welcome in human or elf spaces. If you're looking for a little bit of that elven flavor without trying to wrap your mind around a 700-year lifespan, or if you're interested in exploring the tension inherent in having a foot in two very different worlds, then this is the racial choice for you.

Half-Orc

If the hybrid angst of half-elves intrigues you, but you want a character with more of a heavy metal edge, half-orc may be for you. The result of interbreeding between humans and orcs, the struggle for half-orcs is often two pronged: managing the aggression of their orcish half and coping with many human cultures' prejudice against orcs, thanks to centuries of violent conflict. One thing you should keep in mind if you plan on building a half-orc character, though, is that, thanks to the violent reputation of full-blooded orcs, it has been historically common to portray half-orc characters as the result of sexual assault. This can be a potentially uncomfortable topic to bring up at the table, especially if you don't know your game group well. That's not to say that you shouldn't play a half-orc or even that you can't have a half-orc character with a dark origin story. Rather, I encourage you to approach this topic with thoughtfulness and sensitivity. Sometimes the most memorable characters are those that buck the stereotypes, after all.

If you're wondering why you can play as an elf or half-elf, but only have the option of playing a half-orc, I unfortunately have no good answer for you. Wizards of the Coast have released rules for playing as a full-blooded orc, but they were published in the supplement *Volo's Guide to Monsters* alongside other "uncommon" races and have been reprinted in a number of other rules expansions. My best guess is that, while half-orcs can get by in human cultures despite their appearance, orcs in general have more issues living in civilized areas in many campaign settings. Regardless, while there are rules out there if you want even more orchishness for your PC, since we're focusing on the *Player's Handbook* races in this book, we'll leave our discussion here.

Halfling

Here's a fun fact for you: In the original incarnation of *Dungeons & Dragons*, halflings were called "hobbits." Gary Gygax did not realize that J.R.R. Tolkein had invented hobbits and assumed that, like elves and dwarves, they were a stock fantasy race that any work of fiction could use. This created an awkward situation when Tolkein's estate sent him a cease-and-desist order for violating intellectual property laws. This is why, despite sharing many characteristics with Tolkein's creation, this race is firmly named "halfling" in all subsequent iterations of the game.

Like the hobbits of Middle-Earth, *D&D* halflings are short, unassuming, and have a strong love for the simple comforts of life. They also are preternaturally lucky, having an uncanny ability to get out of tough scrapes. This supernatural luck offsets some of the natural disadvantages that come with being small in a world built for people nearly twice your size. Easy to underestimate, the joy of being a halfling is being able to subvert expectations and use your small stature and unassuming nature to pull off impressive feats of heroism.

Human

A lot of players scoff at the idea of playing a human character. "I pretend to be a human every day when I walk out the door. Why would I choose to pretend to be one for fun?" Ultimately, your character choices are your prerogative. That said, I think there are some strong reasons to play a human that often get overlooked.

Within the world of the game, humans are set apart from the other races by their versatility and drive. They are shorter lived than most other species and, as such, they have a natural inclination towards bold and decisive action. They also are more varied in culture and interest than the other peoples that populate a typical *D&D* world. This means that any kind of character personality will fit a human character without seeming out of place. Playing a human can also be a good choice if you have a strong idea for your character's backstory that you don't want to get muddied by a lot of lore baggage.

Though we're not focusing on the mechanical aspects of character building in this chapter, it still bears mentioning that the specific abilities allotted to human characters make them a race option that is a good mechanical fit for any character class. This is especially true if your DM allows the use of the "variant human" option outlined in the rules. Variant humans are pretty unanimously considered the strongest race choice in the game.

Tiefling

Tieflings are in competition with dragonborn for the weirdest of the core race options and with drow and half-orcs for the edgiest. Much like dragonborn are the result of draconic influence on humanoid bloodlines, tieflings are the result of demonic interference on humans. Tieflings vary widely in appearance, but tend to have strange skin tones, devil-like horns, and, more often than not, forked tails. Because of their wicked appearance, tieflings tend to face a great deal of prejudice within many *D&D* settings, though there is nothing that requires a tiefling player character to be evil. Regardless, this built in character conflict and the angst that comes from having an appearance that is at odds with one's personality has made tiefling a popular character choice, despite its oddness.

Class

Class is the character choice that will have the most impact on how your character operates within the game. In many ways, you can view your choice of race and background as slight variations on your class. Classes represent archetypes from fantasy and other genre stories. Within each class are a handful of subclass options which usually come into play at level 3. These provide another layer of customizability with many of them, especially ones published in expansion books, drastically changing the playstyle of their base class.

Broadly speaking, there are three major categories that classes fall into based on whether they rely on physical abilities, magical skill, or both in combat situations. There's no two ways about it, magic in *D&D* is complicated and many new players tend to shy away from it until they feel like they have a stronger grasp of the rules. I would caution against this attitude. The best character to play is one that you are excited about. If that character is a spellslinger, then that will motivate you to learn the spellcasting system, byzantine as it may be.

Martial Classes

Martial classes are those that rely on their physical abilities and have few or no facilities with magic. Some subclass options can add magical abilities to a martial character's playbook, but even the traits granted by these subclasses generally serve to augment the base class's physical abilities rather than bringing them to the level of the half-caster classes we'll talk about later in this chapter. The four martial classes are Barbarian, Fighter, Monk, and Rogue, each of which presents a different take on the idea of the fantasy warrior.

Barbarian

Inspired by the works of Robert E. Howard (though one could make the argument that the original iteration of Conan is more of a strength-based rogue), the Barbarian is a strong, savage warrior fueled by a berserker-like rage. This rage ability is the central feature of the class, granting a bonus to weapon damage and resistance to physical attacks, as well as other potential abilities through the Barbarian's subclass as they level up.

This is a good class to take if you want to hit hard and shake off big hits in return. Barbarians get more hit points, on average, than any other class on top of gaining abilities allowing them to minimize incoming damage in many circumstances. If you have experience playing video games, this is the quintessential "tank" character. That said, the trade-off is that Barbarians tend to be limited in terms of their options when they aren't able to get up close and personal with their enemies. They also don't get many useful skills or abilities to use outside of combat scenarios, so you may find yourself frustrated during roleplay or exploration, waiting for things to go pear-shaped so that you can do what you do best. The good news is, when it's time for violence, few characters will be more in their element than you.

Fighter

Fighters are the most versatile of the martial classes. As a Fighter, you have the ability to use any and all weapons and armor, meaning that you can be a walking tank with heavy armor and a big broadsword, a nimble, Errol Flynn-like duelist, or a Robin Hood-style archer dealing out rapid-fire arrows from a distance. That's not even taking into account how the various Fighter subclasses can impact your playstyle.

The Fighter has developed something of a reputation as being the "beginner class," especially when paired with the mechanically simple Champion subclass at level 3. While it is true that it's less complicated to play even the most intricate Fighter build than just about any Wizard or Druid, I dislike this stereotype of the Fighter as a "training wheels" class. Each *D&D* class is meant to fulfill a very specific fantasy for the player and there's nothing wrong if your fantasy is being able to absolutely wreck shop with a sword or a longbow. If it weren't a common fantasy, the Fighter wouldn't be one of the only classes present in every single version of *Dungeons & Dragons*.

Monk

While most of the other player character classes are based on figures from the Medieval European fantasy tradition, Monks draw from a very different source. This class is the stuff of kung-fu movies and Shonen anime. A Monk is a warrior that specializes in using martial arts and a wellspring of ki, the essential life-force energy that flows through all living things, to dominate the battlefield.

A Monk may not hit as hard as a Barbarian or have the versatility of a Rogue, but they are experts at battlefield control and dealing with hordes of enemy combatants. Abilities like being able to expend ki to temporarily stun enemies or dish out a bevy of extra attacks make a Monk a potential one-man army. Like the Barbarian, the Monk can often encounter difficulties dealing with enemies over a long range, but no character is going to be perfectly suited for every situation. If you want to live out your Jackie Chan or Bruce Lee fantasies, this is where you want to be.

Rogue

With the possible exception of Bards, Rogues are perhaps the most versatile character class. As a Rogue, you not only get access to the Sneak Attack feature, which gives you bonus damage on your attacks if your target doesn't know you're there or is distracted by another opponent, but also a wide assortment of skills and useful out-of-combat abilities. Rogues are the quintessential dungeon delvers, able to pick locks, search for traps and hidden doors, and avoid detection better than anyone else.

In exchange for this Swiss Army Knife skill set, Rogues can often lag behind other martial classes in terms of damage as their party goes up in level. This is because, unlike Fighters, Barbarians, and Monks, all of whom eventually gain the ability to attack multiple times per turn, Rogues are locked into one attack, albeit with a good chance to do increasingly massive amounts of damage when that attack hits. Besides, there's something undeniably fun in being so absurdly sneaky that even your fellow adventurers have trouble tracking your movements on the battlefield. Plus the rich roleplay opportunities that can arise from the Rogue's assumed criminal connections makes this class a deservedly popular choice among new players and veterans alike.

Half Casters

Though you won't see it used in any official rulebook, "half caster" is a frequently-used fan term to describe classes that, like the pure martial classes, are primarily built to rely on their weapon attacks in combat, but who also get access to a limited amount of spellcasting to augment those attacks and give them more utility outside of their skills with a weapon. Half casters can be a good option for players looking for a little bit of everything that *Dungeons & Dragons* has to offer. They get a good amount of hit points and access to a wide array of weapons and armor while also serving as a relatively gentle introduction to the often confusing spellcasting system.

Paladin

The term "Paladin" is practically synonymous with *Dungeons & Dragons* by this point. Paladins are holy warriors, motivated by a sacred oath; these characters are able to draw on the strength of their convictions to augment their weapon attacks with magical damage. They are also able to bolster their allies in battle and use healing magic to carry out their holy mission.

Paladins have long been subject to the stereotype of being sticks in the mud. Because a Paladin is a literal knight templar, players have often interpreted that to mean that roleplaying one meant having to be a boy scout, not allowed to indulge in the kind of shenanigans that *D&D* parties often engage in. But nothing in the current rule set requires that behavior. The subclass options given to the Paladin are varied in their ethos with some being, if anything, more prone to creating chaos than even Rogues and Bards, who have the opposite reputation to the traditional Paladin. As a result, you no longer need to feel constrained to a certain personality type for your character in order to get access to the ability to smite your enemies with holy light.

Ranger

Rangers can be a bit hard to pin down. The concept behind a Ranger is the ultimate outdoor survivalist. They are warriors who have achieved a level of connection with the natural world that they've gained the ability to supplement their skills with weapons, often bows and arrows, with druidic magic. In practice, though, playing a Ranger can be a bit of a mixed bag, especially in campaigns that don't involve a lot of wilderness exploration.

You see, many of the Ranger's class features have to do with tracking monsters and easing the party's travels across treacherous terrain. The issue is that many DMs don't include these things in their campaign very often, so a lot of these features don't end up getting used. This issue has been lessened with the release of more recent supplements. *Tasha's Cauldron of Everything* in particular included optional alternative and additional class abilities to help the Ranger feel more useful outside of these situations, but the original *Player's Handbook* Ranger can often feel a bit bland because of how rarely they get to do the things that define their class. Don't get me wrong, Rangers can still be very fun to play and as they grow in experience, they get access to many cool, flavorful spells that help fulfill the Ranger fantasy. That said, if you want to play a Ranger, it's probably a good idea to speak with your DM beforehand about whether they're going to give you your opportunity to shine and whether you can use the updated version from *Tasha's*.

Full Casters

Full casters, character classes who rely primarily or entirely on their use of magic spells, can be intimidating to new players. The rules for how spellcasting in *Dungeons & Dragons* works aren't very intuitive, nor are they particularly closely related to any other game mechanic, meaning that playing a spellcaster can often feel like you have extra homework to do when you are new to the game. That said, spellcasting also gives you the ability to influence the game world in ways that you just can't accomplish otherwise, especially at higher levels. As is so often the case in real life, putting in a little more effort can be the key to unlocking unimaginable power.

Bard

Bards derive their magic through the power of art and music. Through the practice of their chosen discipline, they are able to weave powerful spells. They are also gifted with the ability to use their magic to inspire their teammates, improving their odds of surviving a tough scrape. Bards also get proficiency in a high number of skills and eventually gain bonuses even to skill roles they aren't proficient in, making them a useful class to have in the party outside of combat as well.

The current edition of *D&D* has made playing a Bard far more attractive than it had been under previous versions of the game. Bards in the fifth edition are versatile, both when it comes to their options for spell choice as well as their skill utility. The nature of the class lore also means that it's fun and easy to come up with a unique and flavorful idea for a Bard.

Cleric

Much like Paladins, Clerics are fueled by their faith in a higher power. Clerics are the ultimate healing and support spellcasters, a reputation they've had for decades. However, this version of the game also gives them other uses than just dispensing healing magic when their comrades are injured. This comes because, unlike most classes, Clerics get to pick their subclass right away at Level 1. The various subclasses give Clerics access to unique spell options and other abilities.

The upshot of this is that Clerics are, arguably, one of the most powerful classes in the game, able to both dish out damage and keep their party members on their feet. Some subclasses even grant proficiency in armor and weapons, allowing the party Cleric to mix it up on the frontlines, shifting between martial and magical attacks. Overall, Cleric is a consistently fun class choice that can be molded to fit a number of different desired playstyles.

Druid

The Druid is, quite literally, a force of nature. These spellcasters gain their power from a connection with the primal forces of the natural world. This connection doesn't just give them the ability to cast spells, it also gives them the ability to transform into animals. This signature ability makes the Druid, like the Cleric, able to potentially get into melee combat in a way that Wizards and Sorcerers can't.

If there's one thing to be wary of about Druids, it's that they get access to a very large list of spells and can switch out which of these they can cast on a day-to-day basis. This means that getting analysis paralysis as a Druid is a very real concern, even when compared to the Cleric, whose spellcasting works in a similar way. My advice is to not obsess over finding your "optimal" load out right away. Focus on finding a few staples and experimenting with swapping things out only when you find a spell you've had on your prepared list isn't working out the way you'd hoped or when you start recognizing major opportunities that you have to pass up due to not having the right spell prepared. Overall, don't stress. Worst comes to worst, you can always throw spells out the window and just turn into a saber-toothed tiger.

Sorcerer

While other spellcasters come by their powers via intense personal devotion or extensive study of the arcane arts, a Sorcerer is born with innate arcane talents thanks to their bloodline. As such, though their repertoire of spells may be smaller than most other spellcasting classes, they are able to manipulate and alter the spells that they cast to fit different situations in ways no one else can. They can also draw upon their natural magic power to gain additional opportunities to cast their spells each day.

The signature mechanic of the Sorcerer class is called metamagic, a selection of abilities that allow a member of this class to do things like extend the range or increase the power of the spells that they cast. Sorcerers also have the advantage of getting to choose their subclass right off the bat at level 1, making even low-level Sorcerers very distinct from one another. If you have your heart set on playing a spellcaster, Sorcerers can be attractive for the built-in roleplaying opportunities and backstory that comes from being from an interesting family. The fact that they come with fewer spells to memorize and keep track of also makes them a good introductory casting class for newer players or ones who typically play martial characters.

Warlock

Probably the strangest of the core character classes, the Warlock derives their power from bargains made with otherworldly entities. Like Sorcerers, Warlocks pick their subclass right away, reflecting what kind of powerful force is responsible for gifting them with their abilities. As they grow in level, Warlocks get to choose many of the new abilities they gain from a list of options, known as "Eldritch Invocations." This makes the Warlock the most customizable class in the game.

What they are best known for, though, is the unusual way that their spellcasting abilities work. We'll be going into depth on how spellcasting works from a mechanical standpoint for most characters in Chapter

5, but the difference between Warlocks and other spellcasting classes is that they get a much smaller number of spell slots. However, these spell slots recharge after completing a one-hour "short rest," rather than the eight-hour "long rest" that it takes for other classes to regain their spell slots. All of their slots are also of the highest level available to a character of their level, effectively supercharging any leveled spell they cast.

This also has the effect of making them especially reliant on their cantrips, spells that can be cast an unlimited number of times per day, for damage. One cantrip is particularly notorious in *Dungeons & Dragons* circles as the Warlock's bread and butter: Eldritch Blast. This cantrip allows a Warlock to shoot a beam of energy, scoring 1d10 force damage on a hit. As their level increases, they can shoot multiple beams every time that they cast the spell. Any player choosing to play a Warlock should choose Eldritch Blast as one of their cantrips, as it gives their character a consistent source of damage and a sizable number of the Eldritch Invocation options enhance its effect when it hits a target.

Wizard

The archetypal *D&D* spellcaster, Wizards are arguably the most potent spellcasters, having access to the largest number of spells and, at high levels, capable of the most impressive arcane feats, even, potentially, the ability to subtly rewrite reality itself. The trade-off is that Wizards are some of the most fragile characters, having, on average, the lowest hit points of any character Class and lacking any proficiency in armor that could ameliorate that fact. Though there are spells that can make up for some of this deficit in Armor Class, they will still be easier to hit at higher levels than any of their party members. Besides, taking the Mage Armor spell means forgoing other options in the name of gaining a little bit more protection.

Wizards are unique in that they can, theoretically, get access to far more spells than Sorcerers or Bards. This is because a Wizard can expend money and time to copy spells from scrolls or books that they may encounter during their travels. Depending on your DM and how often they make such resources available to you, this may result in you having quite the arsenal to pick from. Of course, the more spells your character knows, the more you, as a player, have to keep track of in order to make sure you're making the most out of your Wizard.

Generating and Assigning Stats

How effective your character is at actually using the abilities given to them by their class, race, and background is largely going to depend upon their stats. These six descriptors of a character's physical and mental attributes determine bonuses for certain skills, attack roles with various weapons, and the potency of a spellcaster's magic. Each stat has an Ability Score consisting of a number from 1-20, though some in-game effects can allow you to increase your stat above this number. Based on that number, each stat also has an Ability Modifier, which can range from -5 to +5, though again, if you encounter an in-game item or other effect that pushes your Ability Score above 20, your Ability Modifier can also exceed its maximum, potentially up to +10. Your Modifier is the number that is actually added to d20 rolls that use the skill as in the damage rolls for weapons and certain spell effects.

The three physical stats are Strength, Dexterity, and Constitution. Strength refers to a character's ability to lift or carry heavy weights, Dexterity to their nimbleness and quickness, and Constitution to their hardiness and health. While Constitution is important for just about every class because it is partially responsible for how many hit points a character gains when they level up, the importance of Dexterity and Strength will depend upon what kind of weapons your character uses and what kind of armor they wear.

The mental stats, Intelligence, Wisdom, and Charisma, can be harder to distinguish. The simplest way to think of it is that Intelligence represents book smarts, Wisdom represents street smarts, and Charisma represents social smarts. All of these traits have associated skills that are important in social encounters or when exploring and investigating. However, these are most important for spellcasters, each of which relies on one of these statistics to determine how effective they are at using their spells. As such, if you are playing a spellcaster, you should always make sure that whichever stat fuels your magic is as high as it can be.

How do you determine these stats? Well there are a number of ways and ultimately it's up to your DM to decide how they want their players to generate them. There is a standard array of six numbers provided in the *Player's Handbook* that is intended as a fair and balanced set of stat numbers that the DM might have each of the players assign to whichever stats they wish. This has the advantage of making sure that all players are on equal footing, though it comes with the disadvantage of practically guaranteeing that every character in the group will have a penalty to one stat, since the lowest number comes with a -1 modifier that can only be eliminated at first level to the detriment of the ability score you like and want to push as high as possible. Even if you accept this negative modifier to one of your stats, the standard array makes it impossible to reach the maximum ability score of 20 at first level.

The most popular method that I have seen used to generate stats is to roll 4d6 and add up the highest three results. Write down the sum and repeat until you have six numbers and assign them to whichever stats you wish. This method is popular because it presents the possibility of rolling several high scores, making for a powerful and multi-talented character. The downside of this, though, is it's also possible to end up with more and worse penalties than allowed by the standard array. Because having both kinds of result in the party can lead to a frustrating imbalance between players in terms of their capability, many DMs institute rules for ensuring that everyone is at least good at what their class is supposed to do and at least okay at one other thing, but this can often result in having to go through the whole stat-rolling process so many times that you might find asking yourself asking for the standard array just so you can get on with the rest of the character building process.

The third, though by far least popular option I have seen is called the "point buy" system. It can be a bit more complicated but it allows players a greater level of customization while still keeping everyone on a roughly even keel as far as power goes. A player has 27 points that they can "spend" on whatever set of six ability scores they wish from 8-15. Higher numbers cost more points than lower ones, with the result being that a player could theoretically spend all of their points to get three of the maximum score allowed by the system while leaving the other three at their minimum, get all of the results fairly even with one another at three 12s and three 13s, or put together a more diverse mix. The reason that 27 is the number of points allocated to each player is because that is the amount required to generate the standard array under this system, meaning that point buy is essentially a more flexible variation on standard array.

However your DM instructs you to generate your stats, once you've allocated them, apply the bonuses provided by your race choice to the relevant Ability Scores or, if your DM is using an optional rule introduced in *Tasha's Cauldron of Everything*, choose two Ability Scores and apply +2 to one and +1 the other. From here, it's just a matter of filling in the skills and abilities you gain from your background, race, and class, adding your proficiency bonus (a flat modifier that starts at +2 and scales up as you gain levels) where it applies and you're off to the races.

Chapter 5: Combat

Although *Dungeons & Dragons* is considered a roleplaying game, it's hard to ignore the fact that the overwhelming majority of its rules have to deal with what happens when resolving conflict with clever words isn't an option and it is time to use violence. This is a fantasy story after all. If *Lord of the Rings* or *Harry Potter* didn't include fight scenes between the characters, they wouldn't be nearly as popular as they are. The reason *D&D* combat involves so many different rules and systems is in the interest of keeping things relatively fair so that a fight is exciting and challenging for the players while still not pitting them against anything so dangerous that they have no chance of victory. This is assuming, of course, that the Dungeon Master is applying the guidelines for constructing fair fights correctly.

As I've said before, the official rules already have, by definition, the clearest rundown of everything you need to know about combat. However, as they can be fairly clinical in their language, I will endeavor to cover the same topics here in plainer language, providing my insight along the way on a few things that can make it easier for you to navigate this important part of the game system your first time out.

Initiative

To keep some semblance of order during a fight, combat in *Dungeons & Dragons* and most other tabletop role-playing games is turn-based. In a combat encounter, each member of the party and each distinct group of enemies roles d20 and adds their Dexterity bonus. This is called an "Initiative check" or, more commonly, "Rolling for initiative." This is meant to determine which characters are quickest to join the fray when it becomes clear that fighting is about to break out. The DM makes a list of all parties involved in the combat in order from the one who rolled the highest initiative result to the one who rolled the lowest. This will be the turn order for this particular combat.

On each creature's turn they can do three things. In game terms, they get an action, a bonus action, and a move action. Each creature also gets one reaction that it can use once per round any time that an appropriate triggering event occurs, whether it's their turn or not. There are also certain things that can be done as a free action on your turn, not using any of these things, but this is a very limited list.

Action

Your action can be thought of as the main thing that you do on your turn. Most spells and weapon attacks take your action to perform, though this is not necessarily true of all spells and there are situations like duel-wielding that can allow you to get a weapon attack as a bonus action. There are also some less exciting options that you can use for your action if the fight isn't going your way and you need some extra protection from damage.

Attack

The attack action is going to be your go-to move in combat most of the time if you are a martial or half-caster class. When you attack with a weapon that you are proficient in, you roll a d20, add either your Strength or Dexterity bonus, depending on the weapon type, and your proficiency bonus and compare it against the enemy's Armor Class. If it meets or exceeds, it's a hit. Roll the weapon's damage die and add the skill modifier from whichever skill you used to make the attack roll (but not your proficiency bonus!) and your attack lowers the creature you hit's HP by that amount. When their HP hits zero, congratulations, you've killed them!

It's important when you're choosing your weapons to remember that, as a general rule, melee weapons, which are weapons meant to be used up close and personal like swords, axes, and clubs, use your Strength modifier in their attack and damage rolls while ranged weapons, like bows and slings, use your Dexterity modifier. The exceptions are weapons with the finesse property. These include rapiers, shortswords, and daggers. Because they are so light, if you are wielding these melee weapons, then you have the option to use your Dexterity in place of your Strength for your attack and damage rolls with them. This is particularly important for Rogues as well as Fighters who are looking to embody the swashbuckling duelist archetype.

There are also two types of special attacks that anyone can take that do not require a weapon and do not deal damage. The first is a shove, in which you attempt to push an opponent away from you or knock them to the ground. The way this works is that you make an Athletics skill check and your target, who must be within five feet of you, makes either an Athletics check of their own or an Acrobatics check. If their result is higher, then they avoid being shoved. If your roll is higher you can choose to either push them five feet back or force them to fall prone on the ground.

The other special kind of attack is called grappling. This is an attempt to grab an opponent to prevent them from being able to move. Like shoving, it involves a contest between your Athletics check and the target's choice of an Athletics or Acrobatics check. The difference is that if you succeed, then your target's movement speed drops to zero and, if they wish to break free of your grip, they must use their action to force you to repeat the skill contest, ending the grapple if they succeed, but wasting their action and remaining grappled if they fail. This can be a handy way to lock down a fast opponent or force a powerful enemy to waste their action on trying to break the grapple.

Cast a Spell

The majority of spells available to *D&D* spellcasters take an action to cast. This is not universally true, of course, as some spells take more or less time, though those that take longer amounts of time don't have combat applications and those that take shorter amounts of time are generally either not damaging or do less damage than spells that take an action to cast. Regardless of casting time, though, any spell follows the same general rules.

In its entry in the *Player's Handbook*, each spell will indicate a number of spell components needed to cast it. The three possible components are verbal, which are magic words or incantations that must be spoken during the casting; somatic, which are complex hand motions that have to be performed; and material, which are physical objects that must be held during the casting to channel the magical energy involved in the process. Material components that do not have a listed monetary cost can be covered by either a component pouch, which is assumed to contain anything you might need for your spellcasting, or an arcane focus, a personal talisman designed to channel arcane energy. Any material component that has a listed cost in gold pieces must be purchased before you can cast the spell and, if the description indicates that the spell consumes that object, you must repurchase the component before each casting of that spell.

Every spell has a level between one and nine. Every spellcasting class has a set of spell slots of specific levels and gains more as the character gains experience and power. In order to cast a spell, you have to expend a slot of the same or greater level than the spell you are casting. In some cases, using a spell slot that is higher than the minimum required by a spell can cause greater effects like higher damage or the ability to target more creatures with it.

The only exceptions to this rule are special spells called cantrips. Cantrips have no level and can be cast as often as you want. Their damage is lower than leveled spells, but does scale up with your character as they gain experience. This allows spellcasters to still have options to contribute in combat even if they've burned through all of their spell slots.

Much like weapon attacks, the efficacy of your spells is partially determined by your stats. Each class has an assigned mental statistic for spellcasting. Wizards use Intelligence; Clerics, Druids, and Rangers use Wisdom; and Bards, Paladins, Warlocks, and Sorcerers use Charisma. Spells that target another creature during combat usually either require the caster to make an attack roll or for the target or targets to make a saving throw. Spell attack rolls work much like weapon attack rolls. Roll a d20 and add the modifier for your spellcasting ability as well as your proficiency bonus and compare the result to the target's AC to determine if you hit. On a hit, roll the damage dice indicated by the spell as well as any other effects that come with successfully hitting. Note that, unlike weapon attacks, spell damage does not include your ability modifier unless otherwise stated by the spell or by a class ability. For a spell requiring a saving throw, the DC for that roll is equal to 8 + your spellcasting ability modifier + your proficiency bonus. Most damaging spells that require a saving throw and which are not cantrips will still do half of their damage if the target succeeds on the save, so that the slot expended is not a complete waste. To determine this damage, roll the spell's damage dice and divide the result by two, rounding down.

There is one final thing to note about spellcasting. Some spells that produce ongoing effects will require you to maintain concentration on them in order to keep them active. You can only have one spell of this nature going at a time and, if you take damage while maintaining concentration on a spell, you must make a Constitution saving throw with a DC of either 10 or half of the damage you have taken, whichever is higher. If you succeed, the spell continues unimpeded. If you fail, the spell immediately ends. This is all the more reason to keep the Wizard as far away from melee combat as possible.

Dodge

The dodge action is the first of several non-damaging options that you can take in combat that can be useful if the enemy is out of range or you find yourself in a situation that is rapidly going south. The dodge action is simple: you assume a defensive stance that forces any and all attack rolls against you before the start of your next turn to be made with disadvantage, so long as you can see your attacker. You also gain advantage on any Dexterity-based saving throws you may have to make during that time.

In most cases where your party is trying to beat a swift retreat, dodging is not going to be your best move unless you are hanging back to try to cover your comrades' escape. Rather, this is something that is most often done when an enemy is out of the range of your attacks and there is no way to reach them during your current turn. Of course, in this scenario, there is another action option available to you.

Dash

Dashing is, in essence, trading your action in for a second move action. So, for instance, if your character, like most *D&D* characters, has a movement speed of 30 feet per round, you can take your move action to run 30 feet, then use your action to dash to move another

30 feet. This is most useful if you are either trying to escape or attempting to close a large amount of distance between you and an enemy.

Disengage

Disengaging is important when trying to escape from a dangerous enemy. When you take the disengage action, it prevents opponents from using their reaction to make attacks of opportunity against you when you leave their melee range until the start of your next turn. We'll go over what some of this terminology means when we talk about reactions, but, for now, suffice to say that using your action to disengage before moving is a good way to get yourself out of a dangerous spot without risking being cut down for your trouble.

Bonus Action

Strictly speaking, you do not have a bonus action in combat unless you have a spell or ability that can be cast or activated as a bonus action. Unlike with actions, there are no universal options for this part of your turn. This also means, it's difficult to discuss what exactly can be done with a bonus action without just listing a bunch of disparate spells and abilities available to different classes and subclasses.

That said, there are a few vital rules to understand regarding bonus actions. The biggest of these is that, if a spell or ability says that it uses your bonus action, you cannot "trade up" and use your action to do it if you've already used your bonus action for that turn. You get one bonus action per round, so use it wisely. This rule exists to prevent some game-breaking combinations of abilities and spells.

The other important and frequently misunderstood rule regarding bonus actions is that, if you used your action to cast a leveled spell, you cannot use your bonus action to cast another leveled spell and vice-versa. Where this rule gets hairy is that there are abilities and spells that can grant a character another action on their turn, such as the Haste spell or the Fighter's Action Surge. If a character is under one of these effects, they can use both of their actions to cast leveled spells, as long as they don't cast a leveled spell for their bonus action. The rule only prevents you from casting a leveled spell for both your action and your bonus action, not from casting two leveled spells in one turn. Also note that you can always cast a cantrip as your action or bonus action (if you have a cantrip with a bonus action casting time), even if you have cast a leveled spell in the same turn.

Move Action

The move action is the simplest aspect of combat in *D&D*. You simply move a distance up to your movement speed. Be aware that you do not have to take all of this motion at once and can split it up in between your action and bonus action. You can even, in some instances, split your movement up in between different parts of your action. For example, at higher levels many martial characters gain the ability to make multiple weapon attacks when they take the attack action on their turn. For example, if the party is in a fight against multiple enemies, a Level 5 Fighter can move 10 feet forward, attack a creature with their sword and, if that creature is killed by the attack, they can then move another five feet to get into striking distance against another opponent and try to hit this second enemy with their second attack.

Reaction

Much like bonus actions, you have to have an ability that is specifically marked as a reaction in order to use a reaction. Reactions also always have a specific triggering condition that must be met in order to use the reaction. Unlike bonus actions, however, there is one reaction that is open to any character with a melee weapon drawn that is triggered when an opponent leaves the melee reach of that weapon. This is called an attack of opportunity and it simply allows you to make a melee attack as your foe runs away from you, provided, of course, that they didn't take the disengage action first.

The other common use of reactions is part of holding your action, which we will discuss in more depth in Chapter 8. Suffice to say that, when you hold your action, you are waiting to act until a specific trigger that you set when you declare that you intend to hold your action occurs. If it doesn't occur before the start of your next turn the action is wasted, including the spell slot if the action you were holding was to cast a spell. Holding your action takes your action on your turn and using a held action once the trigger occurs requires your reaction.

Free Action

Strictly speaking, the term "free action" does not exist in the fifth edition of *Dungeons & Dragons*. However, this was a prominent concept in previous versions of the game and veteran players have continued to use it, even if the rules no longer do. Despite not calling them "free actions" though, there are several activities that you can do on your turn that do not require your action, bonus action, or movement.

The most well-known of these is object interactions. Ordinarily drawing or stowing an object on your person is an action, however you can interact with one object on your turn as part of your move action. This can include drawing a weapon or opening or closing a door. Note that using an object, like a potion, still requires your action and is outside the scope of a simple object interaction.

Beyond this, the other most common "free action" to take in combat is communicating with your squadmates. Obviously, this must be kept within reason. You can't reasonably expect to be able to deliver stirring monologues on every single turn. But you can make brief conversation in order to coordinate with the rest of your party. Ultimately the DM is the final arbiter of this, but as long as you don't try to game the system too much, you should be fine.

In addition, here are some other things that you can do for free on your turn and, in some cases, even when it isn't your turn: you can drop prone on the ground, you can release a creature that you are grappling, you can stop concentrating on a spell, you can drop an item that you're holding, and you can do basically anything that has no mechanical effect on the fight like wink at an attractive NPC who may be watching the brawl or perform an ostentatious flourish with your weapon. There are also some class-specific abilities that don't require any kind of action to complete. These will generally have the phrase "no action required" included somewhere in their description.

This is by no means a comprehensive rundown of every aspect of *D&D* combat, however it is a fairly inclusive overview of the most common things you will encounter and be expected to remember as you become more comfortable with the combat system. Don't be intimidated, though. The cardinal rule is to know how your character's abilities work. As long as you have a reasonably solid understanding of how your character operates when you sit down at the table, anything else can be picked up with relative speed and ease.

Chapter 6: Roleplaying

If the last chapter made you go a bit cross-eyed, you can take heart that, unlike combat, roleplaying is a much looser and more free-form part of the game of *Dungeons & Dragons*. That said, there are some principles to keep in mind when conceiving of your character's personality and translating that idea in your head to the game table. This more than the complicated combat rules is often the hardest part of playing *D&D* for inexperienced players to grasp since, while combat relies on being able to remember set rules, roleplaying involves a level of social intelligence and understanding appropriate behavior.

That said, once you understand how to roleplay in a way that is fun for everyone at the table, this can be many players' favorite part of the game and create some of the best gaming memories. Looking back years later, I don't remember which character got the killing blow in most of the major combats of my first campaign, but all of us can remember the time that the Cleric nearly got herself cooked by trying one too many times to bargain with a Red Dragon.

What is Roleplaying?

When I say "roleplaying," I am referring to all of the in-character decision making and discussion that occurs outside of combat, though even that line can get blurry. More broadly speaking, any time that you are making decisions in accordance with what your character would do rather than what you the player gauge to be the optimal move, you are roleplaying. But this begs the question "How do I know what my character would do?"

The game has a few built-in mechanics to help guide you in this regard. The most famous of these, which has existed in some form since the beginning of *Dungeons & Dragons*, is alignment. You've probably seen the three-by-three alignment grid before. A few years ago it was popular on the internet to post an alignment grid with each entry filled in with a character from a movie or TV show. If you aren't familiar, alignment is an attempt to describe a character's morality via a two-word descriptor that rates them on the axes of good vs. evil and law vs. chaos. A character that is good can be expected to help others, while an evil character will exploit others to further their own ends. Lawful characters have a code of conduct that they respect and hold themselves accountable to, while chaotic characters are ruled by their own passions. Neutrality on either of these axes means that a character has no strong inclination one way or another and may act in ways befitting both sides of the axis depending on the situation.

While it is a classic part of *D&D*, personally I don't find it particularly useful as a roleplaying tool. In past versions of the game there were more mechanics that directly interacted with alignment, but, as it stands, these effects in the current edition are limited to most being requirements for using certain magic items. Personally, when I DM I don't use alignment for any NPCs that I create and, as a player, I only assign one if the Dungeon Master requests it. I just don't think it's an especially useful way to think about what a character would do in any situation, as it's overly simplistic and doesn't account for any number of common edge cases.

I personally prefer to base roleplay off of the "Trait/Ideal/Bond/Flaw" system that we detailed in Chapter 4. This system puts the focus on your character's life priorities rather than a concept of good and evil that can be difficult to pin down. It also gives Dungeon Masters more to work with in terms of engaging the characters on a personal level. If the party is at a tavern and finds out that one of the townspeople was kidnapped by goblins, the party might decide to help out of altruism or because a reward is offered, despite having no personal stake. If, on the other hand, the kidnapped person is the Fighter's younger sister and his bond is that he is "fiercely protective" of her, then suddenly this fairly basic low-level adventure has become much more engaging.

Rules for Roleplaying

One of the tricky things about roleplaying is that, by and large, there are no formal rules for it, especially when compared to the extensive rules that exist for combat and character creation. As far as roleplaying goes, the "rules" are closer to implicit guidelines. Because of this, as a new player, it can be hard to get a grasp on what is and isn't allowed when it's time to start roleplaying.

The key here is to talk to your Dungeon Master about what they do and don't allow at their table. Though there are common trends, the DM is the final arbiter of what can go on at their table. I can guarantee you that every roleplay rule of thumb can and has been broken without ruining the game for the players, even enhancing it in some cases. It all depends on communicating beforehand.

That said, there are things that are rarely allowed and certainly shouldn't be done if you aren't sure whether they are acceptable within your group. Foremost amongst these is intraparty conflict that escalates to the level of theft or violence. This undermines trust and cooperation amongst the group and can be a kind of bullying. It can also be uncomfortable to get into graphic detail about sexual situations, particularly if you are playing with people whom you don't know very well.

Generally speaking, a good DM will have a conversation with a group before the game starts about what is and isn't allowed. I've been running the game for my current group for years now and we still have these occasional check-ins about what we all are and are not cool with. And I can say that, as we've gotten to be closer friends, those parameters have shifted and expanded. Roleplaying is ultimately a trust exercise and, as such, the level of comfortability within the group determines what is and isn't off limits.

Speaking in Character

If you don't have acting or improvising experience, one of the most daunting things about playing a roleplaying game can be having to speak in character. You might feel silly doing it, especially in front of people that you don't know very well yet. It is important that you feel comfortable when you sit down to play. It is totally understandable that you might not be comfortable doing a fake accent and pretending to be a gnome your first time playing *D&D* with a group of loose acquaintances. That said, speaking in character can be a sizable part of the fun and it is worth expanding your comfort zone as you get more accustomed to the gaming environment.

For a lot of players for whom this in-character dialogue does not come easily, one of the first steps here can be simply changing the way that you describe your character's actions. Instead of saying "Marius draws his sword," say "I draw my sword." This is a little thing, but it can get you started on thinking as your character, not as a third-party observer maneuvering them like a chess piece. Once you start putting yourself in your character's shoes, it becomes easier to start speaking for them as well.

Ultimately, speaking in character has very little to do with being able to do an accent or make the rest of the players laugh. If you can do those things and it enhances the experience for you, then that's great. But the reason that being able to think and speak as your character is important is that it is about being fully mentally present within the game so that you can react honestly and within the parameters of your character's personality. This makes for better storytelling and, ultimately, a better gameplay experience.

Benefits of Roleplaying

When you look at the history of *Dungeons & Dragons*, not in terms of just companies and publishing, but in the way the game is actually played, roleplaying's increase in importance is what has marked the evolution of *D&D* from an idiosyncratic twist on the centuries-old concept of the wargame into a new kind of past time. I'm a firm believer that one of the reasons why this new genre of game has gone on to completely overshadow the wargaming genre that birthed it has to do with the psychological and social benefits of roleplay. If you can think back to when you were a child, you probably can remember playing games of pretend that cemented friendships with your playmates. As we get older, this kind of fun can fall out of fashion, but our ability to form bonds through make-believe remains and can be activated by roleplaying games.

Studies have suggested that memories of what happens at the gaming table are filed in the part of our brain that maintains memories of the things that happen to us, rather than the stories that we are told, which is where our memories of movies and TV shows that we've seen or books that we've read are stored. This is why roleplaying games are such a great social activity and can bring people so close together. While you may not actually be fighting demons with your friends, your brain nevertheless associates moments of excitement and adventure with being with your gaming group. Given how difficult it can be as an adult to form close friendships, having a group of close friends can be a major boon to your mental health, even if those friends were made while pretending to be dwarves and elves.

In addition, roleplaying games can be an excellent outlet for people to explore different identities, making them great for building empathy and understanding for the struggles of different groups. This can also lead to personal self-discovery. I don't think it's a coincidence that a large portion of the new or returning players to the hobby since the advent of the new edition brought about a *D&D* renaissance are LGBT+. In fact, for many of these players who I've met and spoken with, part of their recognizing or coming to terms with their identity came from roleplaying as a character of a different gender or sexuality and becoming comfortable with it in that way.

Obviously, not everyone's roleplaying experience runs as deep as this. For most people, it's just fun to get caught up in the story and maybe practice some accent work. But regardless of whether it brings you closer with your friends and leads to personal epiphanies or it just provides you with some fun and escapism, roleplay is a vital part of *D&D*. To ignore or shy away from it is, in essence, to only get half of the experience.

Chapter 7: Being the Dungeon Master

If you're starting completely from scratch with your group of friends who are all new to *D&D* or if you've been playing for a while and found yourself getting curious about running the game, it's likely that sooner or later you will find yourself sitting behind the Dungeon Master's screen. Being a DM can seem intimidating at first. You're in charge of keeping the story moving, after all, and you have to deal with all of the players' wacky hijinks and figure out how to keep them from unraveling the whole game into chaos. How are you meant to juggle all of those balls and keep everything going smoothly?

The good news is that there are countless resources available to would-be Game Masters, tackling everything from remembering rules to prepping sessions and even managing the social aspects of the group as they intersect with the game. This means that, even if you have never even played before, you can go into your first session and still have a good and relatively stress-free time, provided that you understand exactly what is required of you.

In-Game Responsibilities

On a fundamental level, your main job as the Dungeon Master is to make sure that everyone is having fun playing the game. As long as that is accomplished, you are succeeding at being a DM. However, it's important to remember that that includes you. While being a Dungeon Master comes with a bigger workload, you should still be enjoying sitting at the table with friends and telling a good story. But, what exactly are these extra responsibilities that you agree to take on when you agree to be the DM?

Directing the Story

Though all of the players bear some responsibility for shaping the plot of a game session, the Dungeon Master is the greatest contributor in this regard. As the DM, you present the party of adventurers that your players portray with objectives in the form of quests, the pursuit of which will inevitably lead them to encounter obstacles, often in the form of monsters that must be slain, puzzles that must be solved, and any number of other complications.

If you are running a pre-existing adventure module, then it is simply a matter of familiarizing yourself with the story and having the proper information on hand to run the party through the various encounters that will occur on their journey, perhaps coming up with some contingency plans for what might happen if they deviate from the expected course of action. Of course, if you are running an adventure of your own design, then you have to come up with this all by yourself. Once you have a good handle on the rules of the game and what a typical gaming session looks like for your group, this can be a fun, creative project. But, if you are still getting used to *Dungeons & Dragons* as a whole or to your role as Dungeon Master, it can be nerve-wracking. Writing a *D&D* adventure is not the same thing as writing a short story or even a script. There's no singular right way to do it and every DM I've spoken with has their own unique style and method for arranging their notes.

For this reason, I suggest that, at least for your first couple of times out of the gate, you pick up a pre-written adventure so that you can focus on learning how to run the game, rather than learning how to DM and how to design an adventure at the same time. Your players will have a better time and you will feel infinitely more sane.

Controlling NPCs

One of the most important things that a DM does is creating and controlling the non-player characters that populate the game world. This includes everyone from the ordinary tavern keeper at the bar where the party meets to the malevolent dragon they'll have to fight in the final room of the dungeon you plan to have them explore. Depending on an NPC's intended role in the story, the amount and type of prep that you'll have to do for them will vary. If you don't anticipate the players doing much more than talking to them, then you just need to worry about a personality and, if you're up for it, maybe a distinctive description and/or voice for them.

If, however, you anticipate these NPCs becoming involved in combat situations, whether as the players' ally or their enemy, it's important to take an inventory of what they can do in combat and potentially even make some quick notes of what strategies they are likely to employ.

For example, two low-level enemies that most parties are likely to encounter at some point are kobolds and goblins. Kobolds have an ability that gives them advantage on attack rolls against enemies that are already in melee range with one of the kobold's enemies. This suggests that kobolds are likely to attack in large groups and dissipate when they no longer have numbers on their side. Goblins, on the other hand, have an ability that allows them to use their bonus action to disengage, making them well suited for hit-and-run tactics, with particularly clever goblins potentially using this ability to lure players into traps by getting their attention and using this ability to continually slip just beyond their grasp, teasing them into a chase.

These are just two common examples. When looking at the stat block for a monster or NPC, always be thinking about how you can employ the abilities in that stat block and the lore given in the sourcebook to make combat involving these creatures memorable and challenging.

Arbitrating the Rules

In the very earliest incarnations of *Dungeons & Dragons*, the Game Master was simply referred to as the "Referee," as that was a term familiar to the wargamers who were the target market for the original set of pamphlets. Though the game has evolved and become more complex and, in most cases, its goals more lofty, nevertheless, as the Dungeon Master, a large part of your job is making judgment calls on the rules as they relate to what your players want to accomplish.

To be perfectly frank, this is one skill that is easiest to learn by doing. Once you have a better handle on the rules, you'll naturally feel more confident making these rulings as they come up in the game. You'll find yourself able to recall rules on things like combat and spellcasting off the top of your head more consistently and accurately. You'll also develop an intuitive sense for things like when calling for skill checks is appropriate and when it slows down the pace unnecessarily. For now, remember that there's nothing wrong with pausing the action if you need to confirm something in the book and that, when in doubt, a skill check should only be necessary if what the player is attempting is at least reasonably difficult and if the possibility of failure has potential to enrich the story, or at least will not keep them from being able to advance the plot.

Out-of-Game Responsibilities

As important as the DM's in-game duties are, the things that a Dungeon Master does away from the table are perhaps more important to understand if they want to be truly great at running the game. Remember that ultimately your job is to make sure everyone is having fun, which sometimes comes down to the game itself and sometimes has more to do with the environment surrounding it.

Setting Expectations

If you've done any poking around on the internet, you've probably encountered a litany of RPG horror stories. These purportedly real accounts of how gaming has gone disastrously wrong, usually due to issues of human interaction rather than anything to do with what has actually occurred within the game, can be disheartening and anxiety-inducing to anyone new to the community. You don't want to end up having to deal with this kind of awkwardness and, if you're the DM, it's expected that, if things get uncomfortable, you bear the responsibility of addressing the issue.

Let me start by saying that, if you are playing with people that you already consider at least casual friends, the odds of having anything catastrophic happen on this front are fairly minor. You might notice, if you take a closer look at these horror stories, that nine times out of ten, they take place in groups that form out of circumstance rather than organically. Second, even in groups that do form out of strangers who all want to play *D&D* but can't put together a group of their own, most of these problems can be headed off at the pass by having a conversation with the whole table before the game itself begins to set expectations for what you will and will not tolerate as far as player behavior.

Even so, as the DM you should always start off with a new group by laying out what you are and aren't going to allow at your table. You should also allow for a way for your players to communicate what kinds of play they are and aren't up for. It can be awkward and vulnerable to discuss these things, but laying everything out on the table, so to speak, can save a lot of awkwardness and potential drama down the line. A good 90% of problems, both in *Dungeons & Dragons* and in life in general can be avoided by just being willing to have a difficult conversation.

Dealing with Problem Players

Another of these difficult conversations that Dungeon Masters often avoid to the detriment of their game has to do with problem players. These are those players that are disrespectful of the integrity of the game in some way. They might hog the spotlight or make the other players uncomfortable. They also might try to undermine your control over your game. Regardless of the nature of the problem, these players can destroy a gaming group if they aren't dealt with.

The first thing to do is to have a conversation with the problem player. Let them know what about their behavior isn't appropriate and how it is hindering the game experience. Be firm and honest with them, but allow them an opportunity to change. A lot of times people don't realize how their words and actions are perceived by others and, when they are made aware, they can and do make efforts to change their behavior.

If they won't listen, though, you have to be prepared to kick them out of your gaming group. If the way they're acting poses an existential threat to the other players' fun, then it is unfair to keep them around at everyone else's expense. That is a surefire way for your game to collapse. As unpleasant as it can be to lay down the law, it's part of your role as the DM to determine who is and isn't allowed to sit at the table. Remember that the cardinal rule of *D&D* is that everyone should be having fun. If that isn't happening, it falls to you to do what has to be done to fix it. Because if it's not fun for everyone, then what's the point of even playing?

Chapter 8: Advanced Rules and Common Mistakes

Though the days of the Beginner/Advanced split are far behind us, there are undeniably some rules and game systems that either get forgotten, ignored, or incorrectly applied by most tables. Though there's obviously no problem with simplifying your gameplay experience or houseruling it to fit your group's tastes, in many cases players and Dungeon Masters don't even realize that this is what they're doing. In view of that, I'd like to take a moment to call out these mechanics here so that, if it feels like something is off with your table, you might be able to more easily diagnose and remedy the problem.

Held Actions

The rules-as-written allow you to, if you so desire, hold your action in combat until something happens to set it off. This most often happens if an enemy has temporarily gone invisible or hidden and you are waiting for them to reappear. Doing this takes both your action and your reaction and, if you use your reaction for anything else, you lose your held action.

Players can often abuse this ability to unleash massive barrages of damage in a full-party onslaught, killing an enemy with ease before they've had a chance to do much of anything. While this is an intended potential consequence of smart utilization of held actions, there are a few things about held actions that often get overlooked that makes them a little less of a gamebreaker when handled as intended.

The first thing to call out is that there is a reason that this mechanic is called "holding your action" and not "holding your turn." The current edition of *Dungeons & Dragons* only allows you to delay your action in this way, not your whole turn. So the Warlock cannot wait for the Drow Assassin to emerge from their hiding place to use his bonus action to shift his Hex spell over to the assailant and then use his Eldritch Blast as an action, nor can the Barbarian use her reaction both to move to where the enemy appears and attack them with her battleaxe. Held actions are meant to go off in a split second, not to take as long as full turns.

In a similar vein, holding your attack can and should come with some trade-offs. At higher levels, many martial classes gain the ability to attack multiple times when they take the attack action. When you hold your action, the rules indicate that you can only attack once when your reaction is triggered. As such, during higher-level play there is meant to be a potential downside in terms of total damage output if you forgo unleashing your barrage on visible enemies to wait out one that is in hiding.

Similarly, many Dungeon Masters fail to remember a few important drawbacks to casting a spell as a held action. The first of these is that holding a spell takes your concentration, meaning that, as with any other concentration effect, taking damage can cause your concentration to drop and the spell to be lost. This also means that holding a spell, even one that would ordinarily not require your concentration, causes you to drop concentration on any spell you might already have been concentrating on, since you can only maintain concentration on one spell at a time. Finally, and most cruelly, once you have committed to holding concentration on a spell, if it isn't a cantrip, the spell slot is spent, meaning that if you lose concentration or the trigger for your held action doesn't go off before the start of your next turn, the slot is wasted. Much like the restriction on martial attacks, this is meant to cut down on the pile-on of damage when the whole party holds their action waiting for the same trigger, as well as forcing spellcasters to weigh the risks and benefits of holding a leveled spell.

Surprise

Much like held actions, the process of surprising an enemy functions much differently when handled as the official rules prescribe compared to how many groups handle it in practice. Contrary to popular parlance, fifth edition has no real concept of a "surprise round" when the party gets the drop on a group of enemies. The way this is supposed to work is that, assuming conditions allow, the party makes a Stealth check against a Perception check by each of the enemies that they're trying to sneak up on. Anyone who fails this contest is considered surprised. After resolving which enemies are surprised, Initiative is rolled as normal and the first round of combat commences, with any surprised enemies unable to move or take actions or reactions for that turn.

Contrary to popular belief, attacks against surprised creatures do not automatically have advantage. The reason for this misconception is that being hidden from an enemy does grant advantage on attack rolls against them, however, under normal circumstances, emerging from your hiding place to approach an enemy means that you are no longer hidden from them, as does making an attack roll against them from your hiding spot. So, while a Rogue sniping from the shadows with a crossbow might get advantage in addition to surprising his enemies, the Paladin charging forward with their sword aloft would be anything but hidden, even if they have surprised their opponents.

Death and Dying

If you are fortunate, the risk of player character death is one that will rear its ugly head only occasionally at your gaming table. But the result of this rarity is that, in many cases, your DM may not be 100% up on their knowledge of the mechanics behind dying, leading to mistakes that can often carry dire consequences for the players.

The basic idea is pretty simple: when a player character or NPC that the DM has decided merits importance drops to zero hit points, they do not immediately die, but rather fall unconscious. The exception to this rule is if they are brought to zero by an effect whose leftover damage after knocking them out is greater than or equal their total hitpoints. In that case, the character is instantly killed. Once unconscious, at the beginning of their turn, the character has to roll what is called a death saving throw. This is a d20 roll with no modifier, though it does count as a saving throw and thus can be bolstered by effects like the Bless spell. A roll of 10 or higher is considered a success while a roll of less than 10 is a failure. If the character rolls three successes before they roll three failures, they remain unconscious but are considered to be in stable condition unless they take additional damage, in which case the process begins again. If they roll three failures first, though, the character dies. A roll of 1 on the die counts as two failed death saves while a roll of 20 causes the character to rally and come back to consciousness with a single hit point.

Because of the rarity of this last instance occurring, many players forget that, per the rules, a death saving throw occurs at the beginning of the character's turn. Meaning that if they rally, they still get a full turn to potentially heal themselves and/or take some sweet revenge on the creature that knocked them out.

The other major source of confusion is how getting hit while unconscious works. An unconscious creature also has the "prone" condition and the two interact in interesting ways. All attack rolls on unconscious creatures are made with advantage, but ranged attack rolls have disadvantage against prone targets. Since the two cancel each other out, a ranged attack against an unconscious creature is a single roll, while a melee attack has advantage. Furthermore, a hit against an unconscious target counts as a critical hit only if the attacker is within 5 feet of them, meaning that an attacker wielding a weapon like a halberd, which has a longer melee reach, still has to get right next to an unconscious target to have the potential for their attack be a critical hit, though they'd still get advantage on the attack roll from 10 feet away. A critical hit against an unconscious target counts as two failed death saves while an ordinary hit counts as only one failure.

The last thing to note, which is rarer for groups to misunderstand, is that becoming stable or regaining hit points and returning to consciousness resets the death save counter on a creature. So, even if they get knocked out again, a character still has potentially as many as five rounds to make three successful death saving throws, assuming that no one heals or stabilizes them with a healer's kit first.

These are by no means the only obscure or often misunderstood rules in the game, but they are the most often mistaken and the ones whose misapplication carry the greatest potential consequences at the table. As I've said repeatedly, if you're looking for a comprehensive run down of every single rule, that's what the core rulebooks are for. For smaller and non-rules related beginner questions, though, Chapter 11 of this book will serve as a final "Frequently Asked Questions" that may have the answer you are looking for.

Chapter 9: Beyond Your First Session

As you've probably intuited by now, a *D&D* story is usually not constrained to a single evening's worth of play. A campaign, a word lifted from *Dungeons & Dragons'* wargaming roots, is an extended story in which each game session follows in continuity with the one before it. Unlike a "one-shot," a campaign provides characters with the opportunity to grow in power and experience a deeper, often more epic, plot than can be contained in just one session of play. We've already touched on what some aspects of playing these more powerful characters entails, but let's focus in on what going beyond the first session can mean for you.

The Campaign at the Table

Playing in a long-term campaign can create a more relaxed vibe at the table, because not only does playing together over a long stretch of time bring people closer, but the characters they control can reach a greater level of synergy, both in combat and roleplay. Getting a feel for your character's personality can often take a few sessions of gameplay, so after five sessions or so, the party as a whole will usually have reached some level of comfortability, allowing for deeper, more meaningful roleplay and the opportunity for character development. This kind of long-term commitment means that the DM can also create opportunities to directly fold aspects of your character's backstory and personal goals into the plot of the game.

But in order to help facilitate this more complex narrative, it behooves you as a player to take the game more seriously than you might if you knew you were only going to keep this plot going for one to three sessions. This often means having to take more detailed and extensive notes regarding the plot points and characters that the Dungeon Master introduces. This will allow you and your character to participate more fully in the story from week to week, rather than just being a silent figure that comes to life when combat happens and there's a clear goal that can be solved through violence.

In fact, if I had to put a finger on the main difference between playing a one-off, self-contained session, and a long-term campaign, it's that roleplay becomes a larger portion of the time spent at the table. A story contained within a single session, by definition, has a simpler, more action-driven plot, whereas an episodic story is naturally going to have more ebbs and flows to it. A one-shot that contains no combat is difficult to pull off in a narratively-satisfying way, but in a longer campaign, you may have many sessions in which Initiative is never rolled. For some of you, this might sound boring, but you would be surprised how edifying it can be to experience this kind of slow-burning ramp up to a big event. If a one-shot is like an old-school action movie, then a campaign, in its best form, is prestige television. If you adjust your expectations along those lines, it can be a wonderful new form in which to enjoy and participate in the creation of a story.

Second Level and Beyond

However, engaging in this long-form play also opens you up to aspects of character creation that you may not experience in a one-off game. Characters in *Dungeons & Dragons* grow in power the more adventures they experience. This experience is measured by their character level. Usually characters start out as level 1 and max out at level 20 under the official rules of the game. The DM can either moderate the rate of a group's leveling either by dispensing experience points or "XP," a reward for succeeding in combat or advancing the plot in other ways, which trigger an increase in level when certain thresholds are met or else simply use a system called milestone advancement. Put very simply, under milestone advancement, the DM decides when the group gains a level based on meaningful achievements and story advancement. This method has, based on my experience, been gaining in popularity, as it requires less bookkeeping and accounts for the importance of non-combat action in a way that is easier to grasp than the XP system, which, while it does provide some support for non-combat experience, is not very detailed in how best to dole it out.

Leveling Up

We've said that leveling up means an increase in power for your character, but what does that mean in practical terms? Well, the most obvious answer can be found in the portion of the player's handbook that details each class's abilities. Each class entry provides a handy chart displaying which features each class gains at which level. Looking at it, you'll notice that all characters gain increases in their proficiency bonus at regular intervals, increasing your bonus on skill checks, attack rolls, and saving throws with which your character is proficient. Spellcasting classes also gain more spell slots and, along with them, access to more potent forms of magic that can dish out more damage and cause more fantastical effects. All martial classes either gain the ability to make more attacks on their turn or to deal more damage with their attacks. All characters gain more hit points with each level, making them capable of withstanding more punishment in addition to meting out more damage.

In terms of further customizing your play experience, all classes, aside from the Cleric and the Sorcerer who pick theirs at first level, get to choose a subclass at second or third level. These options, enumerated in the *Player's Handbook*, *Xanathar's Guide to Everything*, *Tasha's Guide to Everything*, and a handful of the setting books, each give your character access to a suite of traits and abilities unique from characters of the other subclasses and can, in some cases, even significantly alter the way your character operates in combat.

Multiclassing

Another way to significantly alter the way your character functions in combat is via multiclassing. Multiclassing is technically an optional mechanic, though most DMs I've met allow it in some way, shape, or form. As the name suggests, multiclassing is a method by which your character can gain levels in a class besides the one that they started the game in. In order to do this, a character must meet certain stat requirements in both their original class and the class they wish to multiclass into. This is generally an ability score of at least 13 in the one or two stats most crucial to using these classes' features.

Multiclassing can be a tricky proposition and one that I don't usually recommend to beginners. While a multiclass character can result in a significantly more powerful character than a single-classed character of the same level, some combinations can also be significantly under-powered, making for a frustrating play experience. There are any number of treatises in various corners of the internet about what these optimal and suboptimal combinations are and at what point it is best to start multiclassing, if you choose to go this route. For simplicity's sake, if the power level of your character is something that is important to you, I urge you to think long and hard about how the abilities of your new class will synergize with the abilities of your original class. Also consider that multiclassing can slow down things like your rate of spell progression and the rate at which you gain the ability to multiattack. Of course, if you are more concerned with creating a character with a unique bag of tricks, regardless of how well those tricks coalesce into an optimized whole, then go crazy. *D&D* is not about building the most optimized character, after all, it's about building a character that you enjoy playing.

Chapter 10: The Wider World of Tabletop RPGs

The more D&D you play, the more you might find yourself exploring the wider RPG space. There's only a finite amount of time that you can spend at the table in any given week and, if you get bitten by the bug, odds are that it won't be as often as you'd like. Thankfully, there is a wide array of *Dungeons & Dragons*-related media which can be both a source of enjoyment in between sessions as well as a resource for new things to try with your gaming group. Beyond that, there are also other tabletop RPGs that you might want to consider exploring once you've become comfortable with D&D.

The D&D Community

A sizable portion of the reason for the current *D&D* boom is the explosion in the size of online communities discussing the game, as well as "actual play" media. This term refers to videos, livestreams, and podcasts documenting actual campaigns. There are hundreds if not thousands of these projects out there, so any list of recommendations is going to exclude many pieces of media of equal or better quality. That said, as far as actual play *D&D* projects go, the three biggest names, as of this writing, are probably *Critical Role*, *The Adventure Zone*, and *Dimension 20*. While there are plenty of hidden gems to be found out there, these actual play products have large, engaged fan communities which can be a good way to connect with other *D&D* players. Many of these communities on Reddit and similar online spaces will host regular "looking for group" threads if you don't have enough game time on your calendars.

Another advantage to watching or listening to actual play content as a Dungeon Master is that it can be a good way to both help familiarize yourself with the rules as well as pick up some higher level DM tips. Youtube can also be a great resource for this, as there are many high-quality channels that make videos both on rules topics and on the philosophy behind running a quality tabletop gaming session. The fact that the internet has made this kind of information so easily shareable means that it has never been easier to become a good Dungeon Master and also that quality dungeon mastering is easier to come by than ever before.

Beyond D&D

As we've covered, *Dungeons & Dragons* is the game

that launched the entire tabletop roleplaying game genre. But, despite what most outside observers and even many people within the *D&D* community seem to think, TTRPGs truly are a genre. Though *D&D* is the entry point to the hobby for most people, it is not the be all and end all. If you are like most people, at some point or another, you are going to want to experiment with another game. Although this book is about *Dungeons & Dragons*, it is still worth taking the time to discuss why it's worth exploring the wider world of TTRPGs and a few of the more popular systems to check out if you are looking to expand your horizons.

For many long-time players, inevitably an urge sets in to want to experience a different type of story. The issue is that, despite being the most famous tabletop game system, *Dungeons & Dragons* is not even close to the most versatile. It is designed to tell stories in a very specific genre of heroic fantasy in which combat is one of if not the main plot-driver. It can be stretched slightly to accommodate some deviations from this design intention, but after a certain point, it feels willfully obtuse not to explore other options when you are so obviously trying to fit a square peg into a round hole.

But what other options are out there? It's hard to put an exact count on the number of different tabletop roleplaying games that exist, but it's easily in the thousands. This includes many official tie-ins for a multitude of pop culture properties. I would say that a good 90% of the frustrating posts I've seen in tabletop communities on the internet are related to trying to figure out how to make *D&D* into a way to tell stories within very specific universes. Why try to figure out what blend of *D&D* classes will get you closest to making The Doctor, Captain Kirk, or Harry Dresden when there are officially licensed tie-in games for *Doctor Who*, *Star Trek*, and *The Dresden Files* in which the designers have already figured out the best way to model the kind of stories that fit those settings and genres?

But if you're just looking for something new, then your options are even more wide open. Fan of cosmic horror? *Call of Cthulhu* has been around nearly as long as *Dungeons & Dragons* and remains a giant in the RPG industry. Does the idea of melding Westerns with a healthy dose of dark fantasy sound like fun to you? Check out *Deadlands*. How about futuristic sci-fi dystopia? *Cyberpunk*. You want that plus magic? *Shadowrun*.

Do you like the fantasy setting but find yourself wanting more customizations and a more precise rules system? *Pathfinder*, which you might remember originated as a takeoff of *D&D* 3.5, recently released a second edition that has proved wildly popular and represents a fascinating case of divergent evolution, as both it and the current edition of *D&D* can be seen as providing solutions to what each design team perceives the shortcomings of 3.5 with fascinatingly different results.

Now considering that all of these examples are still big

fish within the RPG sphere, they are games that your friendly local game store almost certainly stocks at least the core rulebooks for. There are many more independently produced RPGs representing a wealth of creative worldbuilding and rules design. If you want to fully explore the breadth of what's out there, you can go on DriveThruRPG, the internet's main purveyor of all-things tabletop and find just about any game in print. You can also ask the staff of your FLGS if they have any personal under-the-radar favorites. Finally, the way that I've discovered many of my favorite lesser-known games has been through checking out booths from small presses at conventions. If you have any desire to attend such a gathering, then odds are you can find some very cool stuff that you might never discover otherwise.

Chapter 11: Frequently Asked Questions

By this point, we've covered most of the essential information that you need to know as a fledgling *D&D* player. As with any rich and varied hobby, of course, there will always be new things to learn, but the basics have been covered. However, as is so often the case, there are a few loose questions that don't fit neatly into any of the major topics we've discussed, so I wanted to take a moment before we wrap up to address a few of these. If there's been something burning in your mind that hasn't been covered yet, then read on. It may be covered here.

Who handles drawing the map when exploring?

This is a question with a surprisingly long history. In the early days of *D&D*, in which the relationship between the DM and the players was much more adversarial, part of the players' job was to try to keep an accurate map based on the Dungeon Master's description. However, as with many aspects of this older style of play, this is no longer a standard expectation for a *D&D* group. You may still decide to draw a rough diagram if it helps you picture what's going on, but it's generally expected that if you are confused, the DM will clear up the layout of the space that you are in, possibly drawing it out for you or showing you a copy of their map that doesn't include the notes they have made to themself.

What is the deal with miniatures?

Miniatures are often used by groups that prefer to have a to-scale visual representation of the game. If your group uses theater-of-the-mind instead, then you don't need to worry about minis at all. If your group does use them, then all you need to know is that minis representing all parties involved in combat are maneuvered around a map of the battleground drawn over a one-inch grid. Each square typically represents five square feet of space. As far as the minis themselves, the DM typically provides them or some other marker to signify characters, though some players who paint figures as a hobby may make their own and bring it to each session. This is far from being an expected norm, though, and nothing you should feel pressured to do unless you want to.

Do I really need all of these dice?

Technically speaking, you do not need dice to play *D&D*. If you really don't want to spend any money and your DM and the other players refuse to loan you a set, there are several free dice rolling apps for iPhone and Android devices that can do in a pinch. However, be aware that, as with any random number generator, the results from these apps will never truly be as randomized as a dice roll, which is why many DMs do not allow them at their table. That said, if the DM you're playing with refuses to lend you a set of dice and won't let you use a dice rolling app, then they don't sound like a particularly nice person and maybe you ought to find a more accommodating DM for your first time out.

How long are turns in combat?

Within the fiction of the game, each round of combat is considered six seconds and, rather than every player acting individually one after another, everyone is acting roughly at the same time. The idea is that the initiative system is an abstracted way to keep things orderly and moving. I will admit that, generally speaking, none of this really holds up to too much mental scrutiny, but ultimately it doesn't really matter. The only game system that really depends on this knowledge is spellcasting, since knowing that a round is supposed to last six seconds allows you to know how many rounds a spell with a specific duration will last. A spell with a minute long duration, for instance, will last for 10 rounds of combat.

Should I be worried if I'm the only newcomer in a group of veterans?

The answer to this one is going to depend entirely on the other players involved. Some veterans have very little patience for newcomers while others are always excited to introduce new people to the hobby. Ultimately, be upfront with the DM about it being your first time and they should know whether or not their group is likely to be accommodating.

Should I dress up? Should I use a different voice when speaking in character?

Whenever I'm asked this first question, I know that the person I'm speaking with has very little exposure to *D&D* outside of poorly-researched depictions on television. I've personally never been part of a group in which cosplaying as your character was a done thing, let alone an expectation. As for using a character voice, that's entirely up to you. Personally, I find it fun, but if it makes you uncomfortable or if you just know that you can't do voices, then it's far from necessary. I've been in groups with great players who had a new accent for every new character they played and I've been in groups with great players whose characters spoke with their player's normal speaking voice.

What is too much prep? What is not enough?

For a player, you should come to the table with a basic knowledge and understanding of your character's abilities, but you shouldn't worry about having everything memorized. If that was an expectation, then there'd be no need for character sheets. As long as you aren't constantly looking up how everything your character can do works, you should be fine and, if you're a newcomer, it's expected that there will be a learning curve for your first several sessions until you get in the rhythm.

As far as DMing goes, this is a much harder question to answer. Every Dungeon Master I know approaches preparation a little differently. One DM I play with semi-regularly frequently improvises entire sidequests off the top of his head, while another meticulously plans for and tries to anticipate any possibility. Both are great at running the game, but they're both very different styles. My advice to new game masters is to err on the side of over-preparation until you find what works for you.

Should I try to make my own character before joining, regardless of what the party needs?

There's no single correct answer here. The current edition of *D&D* isn't designed to require a party member to fill one of a set of prescribed roles like the "tank, healer, DPS" model common to so many online video games. That said, if you show up to a session and everyone decides to play a Ranger, then it can be a frustrating session. Since everyone has roughly the same skillset, no one's character feels unique or special. I had this happen to me once and I can say it was one of only two times that I genuinely didn't enjoy playing. What I would say is that it's worth asking what classes everyone else is playing and choosing one that isn't already represented, but don't feel like you can't play a Barbarian because the group already has a front-liner in the form of a Fighter or that you have to play a Cleric because no one in the group has healing spells.

Do I have to be good at math?

All of the math involved in *Dungeons & Dragons* or, indeed, any other well-designed TTRPG, is easy to accomplish. Nothing you'll be expected to do on the fly amounts to more than basic addition and subtraction. In rare instances, you might have to do some really basic multiplication or division, but I struggle to think of an example of this that is more complicated than doubling or halving a number. If you are just very slow at mental math, there's no shame in whipping out your phone really quickly, especially if you're doing something like casting a high level Fireball spell and need to add up the results of 13d6. In short, don't let a little mental math discourage you from trying the game if you really want to. I've yet to meet anyone with math skills bad enough to render them completely unfit to play *Dungeons & Dragons*.

Conclusion

This has been my attempt at putting together a survey course of the basics of *Dungeons & Dragons*. As I've said at many points, writing a comprehensive how-to guide to the game is a bit of an exercise in redundancy, given that that's exactly what *The Player's Handbook* and, to a lesser extent, *The Dungeon Master's Guide* are. That said, I hope that you've been able to take some insight from our discussion here that will help you approach whatever resources you use to enter your first game with greater confidence, rather than staring blankly at the same sentence in the rulebook for several minutes trying desperately to understand what you've gotten yourself into, as I did when I was preparing for my first session.

In many ways, there has never been a better time to get into *Dungeons & Dragons*. More people are playing the game now than ever before and along with that expanded player base has come a wealth of new ideas and content that, thanks to the internet, can be easily disseminated amongst the player base. It excites me to see so many people I would never have expected to have an interest in this incredibly nerdy hobby not only give it a try, but find that it can be more than a fun pastime that provides them with momentary escapism, and can actually add value and meaning to their life and relationships. It is my hope that this is your experience with this game, as it has been mine.

Now get out there. Adventure is waiting.

Glossary

5e: Short for "5th Edition," refers to the current version of the game. You might also see 1e, 2e, 3/3.5e, and 4e used to refer to past editions.

Advantage: A term used to indicate that a d20 roll should be made twice, taking the higher result.

BECMI: Stands for "Basic, Expert, Companion, Masters, Immortals." The series of box sets for *Basic Dungeons & Dragons* that were the introduction to the game for many children of the '80s and early '90s.

Campaign: A series of interconnected gaming sessions that share one overarching story.

Class: The fantasy archetype that a character embodies from which they derive most of their abilities.

Disadvantage: A term used to indicate that a d20 roll should be made twice, taking the lower result.

Dungeon Master (DM, Game Master, or GM): The player in charge of arbitrating the rules of the game, controlling the world and non-player characters, and directing the story.

The Dungeon Master's Guide: One of the three core rulebooks that contains information on how to run the game and plan a campaign.

FLGS: Stands for "Friendly Local Game Store," a specialty shop that sells supplies for tabletop gaming.

Grognard: An old wargaming term, refers to a veteran player, especially one who tends to be grumpy about modern changes to the rules.

Hit Points: An in-game statistic that measures a character's health and how much damage they can take before falling unconscious or dying.

The Monster Manual: One of the three core rulebooks that contains statistics for monsters and NPCs.

Non-Player Character (NPC): Any character controlled by the Dungeon Master rather than one of the players.

Player Character (PC): A character controlled by one of the players.

The Player's Handbook: One of the three core rulebooks that contains the basic rules to the game as well as information on building characters.

Race: The fantasy species that a character is a member of that determines some of their abilities.

The Satanic Panic: A moral panic propagated among certain parents' groups in the 1980s that held that *Dungeons & Dragons*, amongst other pieces of popular culture, was a tool of the devil.

Saving Throw: A d20 roll used to see how a character responds to an enemy spell or similar threat.

Skill Check: A d20 roll made to see whether a character succeeds at a task.

TSR: Stands for "Tactical Rules Systems," the original publisher of *Dungeons & Dragons*, founded by Gary Gygax and Dave Arneson.

Wizards of the Coast (WotC): The current publisher of *Dungeons & Dragons*.

References

Ammann, K. (2019). *The monsters know what they're doing : Combat tactics for dungeon masters.* Saga Press.

Ammann, K. (2020). *Live to tell the tale : Combat tactics for player characters.* Saga Press.

Crawford, J. (2020, April 6). *Sage advice compendium.* Dungeons & Dragons; Wizards of the Coast. https://dnd.wizards.com/articles/sage-advice/sage-advice-compendium

de Kleer, E. (2017, July 25). *How inmates play tabletop RPGs in prisons where dice are contraband.* Vice. https://www.vice.com/en/article/padk7z/how-inmates-play-tabletop-rpgs-in-prisons-where-dice-are-contraband

Ewalt, D. M. (2013). *Of dice and men : The story of dungeons & dragons and the people who play it.* Scribner.

Freedman, I. (n.d.). *What is a free action in D&D?* FandomSpot. Retrieved February 13, 2022, from https://www.fandomspot.com/dnd-free-action/

Kaminske, A. N. (2018, August 23). *Learning in dungeons and dragons*. The Learning Scientists. https://www.learningscientists.org/blog/2018/8/23-1

Mearls, M., & Crawford, J. (2014a). *Dungeons & dragons dungeon master's guide*. Wizards of the Coast.

Mearls, M., & Crawford, J. (2014b). *Dungeons & dragons player's handbook*. Wizards of the Coast.

Mearls, M., Crawford, J., Schwalb, R. J., Sernett, M., Townshend, S., & Wyatt, J. (2014). *Dungeons & dragons monster manual*. Wizards of the Coast.

Waldron, D. (2005). Role-Playing games and the christian right: Community formation in response to a moral panic. *Journal of Religion and Popular Culture*, 9(Spring 2005).

Witwer, M., Newman, K., Peterson, J., Witwer, S., & Manganiello, J. (2018). *Dungeons & Dragons art & arcana : A visual history*. Ten Speed Press.

Made in the USA
Las Vegas, NV
10 September 2023

77390754R00085